'Although the causes of eating disorders are complex, there is no doubt that society's overvaluation of thinness plays a major role. This book provides an important perspective: the burden of challenging unrealistically thin body ideals should not fall solely on the individual and the government has a responsibility to protect the public from harmful images. The author is clearly passionate about the topic and takes the reader through the history, successes, and pitfalls of international law and policy designed to ensure that the mass media do not glorify being underweight. Extremely well researched and eye-opening, this book is a fascinating read.'

Jennifer Mills, *Psychologist and Professor, York University*

'This highly readable book is the first to present a comprehensive analysis of Body Image Law and proposed but unsuccessful law designed to reduce exposure to thin ideal images, including from Israel, France, Norway, US, UK and Brazil. It also provides a unique review of legislation and self-regulation into related areas such as on-line safety and pro-ana websites. A key feature of this work is a balanced critique of research into different approaches and examination of the effectiveness of legislation through the lens of evidence. This paves the way for a fascinating look into future legislative possibilities.'

Susan Paxton, *Emeritus Professor, La Trobe University*

'In this book, Bromberg brings together detailed reviews of current Body Image Law worldwide and the evidence for effectiveness of these laws on improving mental health and outcomes. Despite lack of definitive evidence, the book ends on a hopeful note. Bromberg also points to the alarming increase in the use of artificial intelligence to produce images and highlights the rapidly changing landscape and the likely need for flexible and time-responsive future actions. This book resonates and speaks to all, i.e. scholars, health care providers, policy and law makers and most of all to people experiencing unhelpful body image pressures.'

Phillipa Hay, *Professor and Chair of Mental Health, Western Sydney University*

'Dr Bromberg's pioneering book not only documents international legislative measures and policy initiatives, but also engages in a critical evaluation of their effectiveness. Particularly noteworthy is its nuanced exploration of the interrelated roles of media, prevailing social norms, and industry practices in shaping body image and influencing the prevalence of eating disorders. It draws on doctrinal analysis, empirical evidence, and international comparative perspectives, which is further enriched by valuable annexures. This scholarly and multidimensional approach ensures that the work will be an indispensable resource for academics, policymakers, and practitioners in the fields of public health, media studies, and related disciplines.'

Vagia Polyzoidou, *Associate Professor, University of Nicosia School of Law*

'Bromberg's primer on Body Image Law is an essential read for 2025 – and for anyone working in the broad sphere of online harms. It captures a breadth of law and policy discussions and offers real food for thought without seeking to advocate for distinct policy change in a rapidly evolving area. Importantly, it is written – deliberately – in an accessible manner. This will undoubtedly trigger conversations – conversations that we should all be having. This book marks a line in the sand from which we start those conversations.'

Kim Barker, *Professor, University of Lincoln Law School*

Body Image Law

This book examines the effectiveness and limitations of existing body image law, and proposes evidence-based regulatory alternatives informed by public health and psychology research.

Poor body image affects millions of people worldwide, and, despite the body positivity movement, the pressure on women in Western countries to have smaller bodies continues to cause significant harm to many. This book contributes to improving this, through drawing on evidence from research which outlines the harm excessive social media use and exposure to models with smaller bodies can cause to an individual's body image. It explores the regulatory efforts of governments in Israel, France and Norway which passed Body Image Laws, and failed attempts to pass bills in this area in Canada, the United Kingdom, Brazil and the United States. This book analyses the outcome of BMI requirements for catwalk fashion models, warning messages on digitally altered images and prosecuting pro-anorexia content creators. It asks why the current forms of body image law do not align with significant findings from public health and psychology. This book offers a compelling, evidence-based overview of body image as it intersects with law. It argues that body image law in its current form is unlikely to be effective and makes suggestions for evidence-based approaches instead.

This book will be of interest to researchers concerned with body image and the law as it relates to public health law, social media law and advertising law and anyone who has poor body image, an eating disorder or knows someone who has.

Marilyn Bromberg, FHEA ('M'), is a mother and a dual Canadian and Australian citizen. She is an Associate Professor at the University of Western Australia and a practising lawyer. M was a visiting scholar at STRIPED at the T.H. Chan School of Public Health at Harvard University/Boston Children's Hospital. M has the following qualifications: PhD, LLB (Dist), BBA (Hon), Grad Cert Pop Health Studies and Grad Cert University Teaching. She also plays piano, takes singing lessons and loves being outside. M has a great passion to try to help people who have poor body image and eating disorders using research and advocacy.

Routledge Research in Fashion Law

Protecting Creativity in Fashion Design
US Laws, EU Design Rights, and Other Dimensions of Protection
Susanna Monseau

Artificial Intelligence, Design Law and Fashion
Hasan Kadir Yılmaztekin

Couture Fashion Law
Copyright and Artistic Works
Tomruk Űstűnkaya

Body Image Law
Revolutionising Images of Thin-Ideal Women
Marilyn Bromberg

For more information about this series, please visit Routledge Research in Fashion Law - Book Series - Routledge & CRC Press

Body Image Law

Revolutionising Images of Thin-Ideal Women

Marilyn Bromberg

Routledge
Taylor & Francis Group
LONDON AND NEW YORK

First published 2026
by Routledge
4 Park Square, Milton Park, Abingdon, Oxon OX14 4RN

and by Routledge
605 Third Avenue, New York, NY 10158

Routledge is an imprint of the Taylor & Francis Group, an informa business

British Library Cataloguing-in-Publication Data
A catalogue record for this book is available from the British Library

ISBN: 978-1-041-12967-7 (hbk)
ISBN: 978-1-041-15309-2 (pbk)
ISBN: 978-1-003-67879-3 (ebk)

DOI: 10.4324/9781003678793

Typeset in Times New Roman
by Deanta Global Publishing Services, Chennai, India

This book is dedicated to Kennedy Krawitz, Howard Bromberg and Linda Bromberg (with love). This book is also dedicated to anyone who has ever had an eating disorder and the people who love them (with empathy) and to the eating disorder that I had for over 20 years (with vengeance that fuels my Body Image Law research and advocacy).

Contents

Foreword

With exceptional clarity and global scope, Bromberg maps the emergence of Body Image Law as a distinct legal field: one built to confront the psychological fallout of manipulated visual ideals. She brings together law, mental health, public policy and education in a way that is both scholarly and urgent, showing how outdated regulatory systems are failing a generation trained to compare themselves to digitally altered illusions.

What makes this book truly revolutionary is not just its breadth, but its conviction: that the images we consume are never neutral, and that governments have a role to play in protecting citizens from their toxic effects. This is jurisprudence for the algorithmic era, where the right to self-worth and body authenticity must be defended as vigorously as any civil liberty.

For legal scholars, mental health professionals, educators and interdisciplinary researchers, this is essential reading. For policymakers and advocates, it offers a bold, evidence-based framework for rethinking regulation in the age of digital self-image, and for shaping a more just and psychologically safe visual culture. In doing so, it lays the foundation for what may become one of the most important legal disciplines of our time: body visual jurisprudence.

Dr Anne Wagner, *Centre de Recherche Droits et Perspectives du Droit, équipe René Demogue, University of Lille, France,* & Editor-in-Chief of the *International Journal for the Semiotics of Law.*

Preface

This book contains content about eating disorders and poor body image and related topics. Reader discretion is advised. If you are struggling or may be triggered by this material, please take care and seek support if needed.

A few of the organisations that offer information and support to people who have poor body image or eating disorders are listed below.

Australia: the Butterfly Foundation. The Butterfly Foundation is a national charity for all Australians who are impacted by body image challenges and eating disorders and the people who support them.[1] Butterfly offers evidence-based assistance, resources and treatment that is evidence-based.[2] If you need support with your body image, or with eating disorders, you can contact them on their helpline, 1.800.33.4673, or butterfly.org.au/helpline.[3]

Canada: the National Eating Disorder Information Centre. This organisation is Canada's source for eating disorder education and support.[4] They 'guide people to trustworthy information and resources relevant to their needs'.[5] You can access support, resources and information about treatment options through their toll-free helpline and live chat service.[6] Their helpline and live chat details can be found on their webpage.[7]

United Kingdom: Beat, the UK's eating disorder charity.[8] Beat is a national charity that exists to 'end the pain and suffering caused by eating disorders'.[9] They support people who have eating disorders and the people who love them. You can contact them online or by telephone to get help.[10] Their telephone

1 Butterfly Foundation, 'About Us' <https://butterfly.org.au/who-we-are/about-butterfly/>.
2 Ibid.
3 Butterfly Foundation, 'Get Support' <https://butterfly.org.au/get-support/helpline/>.
4 National Eating Disorders Information Centre, 'Mission' <https://nedic.ca/about/>.
5 Ibid.
6 National Eating Disorders Information Centre, 'Contact NEDIC' <https://nedic.ca/contact/>.
7 https://nedic.ca/contact/
8 Beat Eating Disorders, 'About Beat' <https://www.beateatingdisorders.org.uk/about-beat/>.
9 Ibid.
10 Ibid.

numbers and webchat can be found on the webpage https://www.beateatingdisorders.org.uk/helplines.[11]

United States: the National Eating Disorders Association.[12] They offer resources, education and support research and early eating disorder intervention.[13,14]

11 Beat Eating Disorders, 'Helplines' <https://www.beateatingdisorders.org.uk/get-information-and-support/get-help-for-myself/i-need-support-now/helplines/>.

12 National Eating Disorders Association, 'About Us' <https://www.nationaleatingdisorders.org/about-us/>.

13 Ibid.

14 To get screened and find treatment, visit: https://www.nationaleatingdisorders.org/> and their contact page is: <https://www.nationaleatingdisorders.org/contact-us/>.

Acknowledgements

In about 2012, I read an article in *The West Australian* newspaper about a new law in Israel that would require models to have a minimum BMI, and if an image was altered to make the model look thinner, it required a warning. The article intrigued, amazed and inspired me. I started researching and writing journal articles about how seeing images of a woman's thin-ideal body can impact the body image of some women negatively, and potentially lead to eating disorders. I also wrote about how this connection inspired some politicians to try to use law to address this issue, which Cindy Halliwell and I called Body Image Law.

I extend sincere thanks to all of my biological and non-biological family for their love and support and to listening to me patiently consistently talk about my Body Image Law research since what may feel like the beginning of time (but was really about 2012). Thanks, specifically, to my metaphorical cheerleaders (in first name alphabetical order): Ali Pano, Alicia Savona, Barbara Price, Caroline Odong, Dr Emily Fletcher, Ester Klimitz, Eve Grill, Dr Jenny Lou, Jon Polak, Laura Fitzgerald and Marvin Grill. Thanks, also, to Alicia Savona, Dr Jasmine Fardouly, the Butterfly Foundation and another person who wishes to remain anonymous for reading through this book and providing helpful feedback.

Further, I thank my editors at Routledge, Nicola Sharpe and Diksha Bhugra, for being helpful, supportive and very patient with me.

1 Introduction

Introduction

The *Merriam-Webster Dictionary* defines 'a dog's breakfast', a popular British expression, as 'something that is messy or poorly done'.[1] This unique expression arguably applies to Body Image Law, as it currently exists worldwide. Body Image Law

> encompasses the bills, laws and government actions (such as establishing parliamentary inquiries and creating policies) that may help to improve the body image of the general public, and particularly of young people…Body Image Law can include measures such as: (1) requiring people to have a minimum body mass index ('BMI') to work as models; (2) requiring editors and other relevant people to post a warning on images of people who they have photoshopped to appear thinner; (3) forbidding the altering of images of the bodies of models to make them appear thinner; (4) requiring retailers to sell clothes that come in diverse sizes (including clothes in larger sizes); and (5) forbidding certain words from accompanying images of models or recommending that certain words do not accompany images of models e.g. a government policy that recommends that the words 'plus size' are not placed beside a model's image.[2]

Body Image Law is likely best known internationally for the form that it takes in France, Israel and Norway:[3] those laws require a disclaimer on images

1 *Merriam-Webster* (online at 17 April 2025) 'A Dog's Breakfast'.

2 Marilyn Bromberg and Cindy Halliwell, '"All about that Bass" and Photoshopping a Model's Waist: Introducing Body Image Law' (2016) 18 *The University of Notre Dame Australia Law Review* 2. <https://researchonline.nd.edu.au/undalr/vol18/iss1/1/>.

3 *Code de la santé publique* [Public Health Code] (France) art L223-2-1; *Code du travail* [Labour Code] (France) art L7123-2; *Lov Om Endringer i Markedsføringsloven mv. (Merking Av Retusjert Reklame)* [Act on Amendments to the Marketing Act, etc. (Labelling of Retouched Advertising)] (Norway), 11 June 2021, No. 62; תעצה קוח תלבגה לקשמ ףנעב תונמגודה [Law for Restricting Weight in the Modelling Industry], 27 March 2012, 5772-2012.

DOI: 10.4324/9781003678793-1

of models that were digitally altered to make models appear thinner, and in France and Israel the laws also assess models' health, with particular regard to their body mass index (BMI) (France)[4] or require them to have a minimum BMI to work (Israel).[5]

Before this book can discuss Body Image Law in detail, including why it appears to be a 'dog's breakfast', it will provide important background information to help you understand why it was created and why it is important to research it in depth, critically analyse it and potentially even advocate for it (or more likely a variation thereof). However, if you do not want to read this background information, and prefer to read the legal and policy parts of this book right away, please skip ahead to Chapter 5 (the author enjoyed many a Choose Your Own Adventure novel as a child).

To start, if you think of the ideal woman's body, you may, like many, imagine a thin woman. The media typically presents a thin body,[6] with a small waist and flat stomach, as the ideal.[7] In western culture, a woman's worth is often associated with her body, which must be thin.[8] Being thin may also send a message to the world (albeit an untrue one) that a woman is successful and healthy.[9] Globalisation and social media contributed to spreading the thin body ideal ('thin-ideal') worldwide.[10] The pressure to match the thin-ideal applies to women of different races and ethnicities.[11]

Most advertisements currently feature women with thin and toned bodies that were digitally manipulated and are 'unattainable'.[12] These images often look unrealistically thin initially, but digital altering makes them appear

4 *Code du travail* [Labour Code] (France) art L. 7123-2-1.

5 תונמגודה ךנעב לקשמ תלבגה קוח תעצה [Law for Restricting Weight in the Modelling Industry], 27 March 2012, 5772-2012, ss 1, 2a.

6 Helga Dittmar and Sarah Howard, 'Thin-Ideal Internalization and Social Comparison Tendency as Moderators of Media Models' Impact on Women's Body-Focused Anxiety' (2004) 23(6) *Journal of Social and Clinical Psychology* 768, 769.

7 Sarah E McComb and Jennifer S Mills, 'The Effect of Physical Appearance Perfectionism and Social Comparison to Thin-, Slim-Thick-, and Fit-Ideal Instagram Imagery on Young Women's Body Image' (2022) 40 *Body Image* 165, 165 ('The Effect of Physical Appearance').

8 Diana E Betz and Laura R Ramsey, 'Should Women Be "All About That Bass?": Diverse Body-Ideal Messages and Women's Body Image' (2017) 22 *Body Image* 18, 18.

9 Sharlene Hesse-Biber et al, 'The Mass Marketing of Disordered Eating and Eating Disorders: The Social Psychology of Women, Thinness and Culture' (2006) 29 *Women's Studies International Forum* 1, 1.

10 Britney Clasper, 'Conceptualising a Preventative Approach to Eating Disorders in New Zealand' [2023] *New Zealand Law Students' Journal* 105, 113.

11 Helen Trepal, Yulia Cannon and Jessenia Garcia, 'Using Photovoice to Promote Body Image Resilience in College Women' (2020) 23 *Journal of College Counselling* 44, 44.

12 Elisa S Danthinne, Francesca E Giorgianni and Rachel F Rodgers, 'Labels to Prevent the Detrimental Effects of Media on Body Image: A Systematic Review and Meta-Analysis' (2020) 53 *International Journal of Eating Disorders* 647, 648.

even more so.[13] Digital altering is widespread[14] and it can be difficult for the average person to tell that an image was altered.[15] People used to primarily digitally alter images of famous people, but for some time now anyone has been able to alter an image of any person – and countless people do.[16]

The pressure on women to match the thin-ideal to conform to society's expectations of beauty is merely a recent type of pressure on women to alter their bodies to be beautiful: there is a long history of this kind of pressure, which some researchers argue tries to control them.[17] For example, some of the different measures women took to try to conform to beauty pressures were binding their feet in ancient China and using a corset in the Victorian period.[18]

People who work in the fashion industry often call their top models 'clothes hangers': they wish their bodies were thinner to show off their clothes.[19] This thinking likely contributed to some models starving themselves which led to their deaths, sometimes right after they walked on a runway.[20]

The average international model's BMI is usually below the World Health Organization's 'threshold for medically dangerous thinness for adults'.[21] Many adolescent females and women think that they should look similarly thin,[22] even though there is a significant difference between the height and size of a model and that of a typical woman.[23] Researchers examined women's bodies on the front cover of four fashion magazines from 1959 to 1999:

13 Rachel F Rodgers and Katherine Laveway, 'Retouchée au Féminin: The Gendered Nature of the French Law Mandating Labeling of Digitally Modified Images' (2021) 10(62) *Laws* 1, 2.

14 Allison J Lazard, Mary A Bock and Michael S Mackert, 'Impact of Photo Manipulation and Visual Literacy on Consumers' Responses to Persuasive Communication' (2020) 39(2) *Journal of Visual Literacy* 90, 104.

15 Sophie J Nightingale, Kimberley A Wade and Derrick G Watson, 'Can People Identify Original and Manipulated Photos of Real-World Scenes?' (2017) 2(1) *Cognitive Research: Principles and Implications* 1, 16.

16 Minsun Lee, Hyun-Hwa Lee and Allison J Ouimet, 'Can Virtual Makeovers Using Photo Editing Applications Moderate Negative Media Influences on SNS Users' Body Satisfaction?' (2019) 51(4) *Canadian Journal of Behavioural Science* 231, 231–233.

17 Nicole Danielle Schott and Debra Langan, 'Pro-Anorexia/Bulimia Censorship and Public Service Announcements: The Price of Controlling Women' (2015) 37(8) *Media, Culture & Society* 1158, 1159.

18 Ibid.

19 Katherine L Record and Bryn S Austin, '"Paris Thin": A Call to Regulate Life-Threatening Starvation of Runway Models in the US Fashion Industry' (2016) 106(2) *American Journal of Public Health* 205, 205.

20 Ibid.

21 Ibid.

22 Ibid.

23 Charles R Taylor and Yoon-Na Cho, 'Photoshopping of Models in Advertising: A Review of the Literature and Future Research Agenda' (2018) 9(4) *Journal of Global Fashion Marketing* 379, 382.

Cosmopolitan, *Glamour*, *Mademoiselle* and *Vogue*.[24] They found that fashion models looked increasingly thin in the 1980s and 1990s.[25]

In recent years, women have increasingly wanted to have a body that is different to the traditional thin-ideal.[26] Some seek the 'slim-thick' body ideal: Beyoncé is an example of a woman who has this body type,[27] which consists of a flat stomach, small waist and large breasts and thighs.[28] It is relatively new for a 'slim-thick' body ideal to be popular among white women, but it has been popular with Black and Latino women for years.[29] Another alternative ideal woman's body in recent years is a thin and toned body, rather than just a thin one.[30] Over the past 15 years, increasing numbers of Miss U.S.A. Pageant competitors have had this body type.[31] The thin-ideal is still the most popular body type for women in mainstream media,[32] so this book focuses on it. Whether a woman seeks to be the thin-ideal, 'slim-thick' ideal or thin and fit ideal, there is a commonality among the three body types: they all involve at least being mostly thin and they are all difficult to attain.

In recent years, there have been reports that models are primarily the thin-ideal after years of more diverse models: of the 8,000-plus looks in over 200 female fashion shows in about October 2024, 94.9% were shown on models who were a size 0–4 U.S. (which is equal to size 4–8 U.K.).[33] This change occurred amid the medication Ozempic being increasingly used for weight loss.[34] (This book will discuss Ozempic again in Chapter 9.)

24 MF Sypeck, JJ Gray and AH Ahrens, 'No Longer Just a Pretty Face: Fashion Magazines' Depictions of Ideal Female Beauty from 1959 to 1999' (2004) 36(3) *The International Journal of Eating Disorders* 342, 343–344.

25 Ibid 346.

26 Sarah E McComb and Jennifer S Mills, 'Eating and Body Image Characteristics of Those Who Aspire to the Slim-Thick, Thin, or Fit Ideal and Their Impact on State Body Image' (2022) 42 *Body Image* 375, 385 ('Eating and Body Image').

27 Ibid 376.

28 McComb and Mills, 'The Effect of Physical Appearance' (n 7) 165.

29 Ibid 166.

30 Frances Bozsik et al, 'Thin Is In? Think Again: The Rising Importance of Muscularity in the Thin Ideal Female Body' (2018) 79(9–10) *Sex Roles* 609, 613.

31 Ibid 611.

32 McComb and Mills (n 7) 166.

33 Chloe Mac Donnell, 'Fashion Experts Raise Concern about Return to "Extremely Thin Models"', *The Guardian* (online, 11 October 2024) <https://www.theguardian.com/fashion/2024/oct/11/fashion-experts-raise-concern-about-return-to-using-extremely-thin-models>.

34 Kalhan Rosenblatt, 'Is the Era of Body Positivity over? Some Experts Worry about a Return of "thinness" as the Norm', *NBC News* (online, 29 December 2024) <https://www.nbcnews.com/pop-culture/viral/era-body-positivity-experts-worry-return-thinness-norm-rcna184050>.

While seeing images of thin-ideal models in everyday life may appear, on the surface, to be harmless, it is not: it can contribute to some women developing poor body image[35] and, subsequently, eating disorders.[36]

There is a paucity of research about how seeing images of 'slim-thick' women and thin and toned women can impact viewers,[37] though one study found that seeing 'slim-thick' images of women lowered body image satisfaction.[38] It also found that seeing 'slim-thick' images can threaten women's body image more than seeing thin-ideal images, especially for women who seek 'a perfect appearance'.[39] It also discovered that women who want to have a 'slim-thick' body have disordered eating behaviours similar to women who seek to be the thin-ideal and might be comparably at risk of developing eating disorders.[40]

Researchers also found that women who saw images of women who were thin and fit experienced more body dissatisfaction than women who only saw thin-ideal images.[41] This may be because the thin, fit body could appear more attainable than a merely thin body: women may believe that if they eat healthily and exercise they can achieve it.[42]

A small amount of eating disorder research exists about methods to prevent eating disorders: the majority deals with diagnosing and treating those affected, and their general progressing and developing over time.[43] Passing Body Image Law is a potential macro-level way to help address the connection, for some women, between seeing the thin-ideal and developing poor body image and as a result, eating disorders. You might assume that the Law, if people abide by it, will result in less thin-ideal images for viewers to see. If there are less thin-ideal images, then you might also assume that less women would then develop poor body image and eating disorders. Alternatively, you might assume that seeing thin-ideal images with disclaimers on them (which state that the images were altered to make the models appear thinner or a variation thereof) would stop the images from harming women who might

35 Lisa M Groesz, Michael P Levine and Sarah K Murnen, 'The Effect of Experimental Presentation of Thin Media Images on Body Satisfaction: A Meta-Analytic Review' (2002) 31(1) *The International Journal of Eating Disorders* 1, 11.

36 Eric Stice et al, 'Relation of Media Exposure to Eating Disorder Symptomatology: An Examination of Mediating Mechanisms' (1994) 103(4) *Journal of Abnormal Psychology* 836, 839.

37 McComb and Mills, 'Eating and Body Image' (n 29) 376.

38 McComb and Mills, 'The Effect of Physical Appearance' (n 7) 172; McComb and Mills, 'Eating and Body Image' (n 26) 381.

39 McComb and Mills, 'The Effect of Physical Appearance' (n 7) 172.

40 McComb and Mills, 'Eating and Body Image' (n 26) 382.

41 Lily Robinson et al, 'Idealised Media Images: The Effect of Fitspiration Imagery on Body Satisfaction and Exercise Behaviour' (2017) 22 *Body Image* 65, 69; McComb and Mills, 'Eating and Body Image' (n 26) 381.

42 Robinson et al (n 41) 69.

43 S Bryn Austin, 'Accelerating Progress in Eating Disorders Prevention: A Call for Policy Translation Research and Training' (2016) 24(1) *Eating Disorders* 6, 7.

otherwise aspire to unrealistic body images. Of course, women may develop poor body image and eating disorders from many other factors besides seeing the thin-ideal: there have been thousands of studies on the causes of eating disorders.[44] Some of the causes of eating disorders involve personality, like being a perfectionist[45] or neurotic.[46] Interpersonal experiences (e.g. abuse, trauma and teasing about body shape or appearance) can also contribute to developing eating disorders.[47] Those other factors obviously require quite different approaches to address them. Nevertheless, seeing thin-ideal images can contribute to some women acquiring poor body image[48] and, subsequently, eating disorders.[49]

This book is the only publication (known to the author) that states every single law, bill (a proposed law that has not yet become law) and policy (typically principles to achieve particular goals) in the Body Image Law area. They are from jurisdictions worldwide and relatively new (proposed or passed within approximately the past 20 years). Relatedly, this book is also, somewhat, historical: Body Image Law has an approximate 20-year history and this book describes its main events during this time. The author now turns to the content of the next chapter onward.

This book focuses on thin-ideal images and two of the main limbs of Body Image Law: (1) requiring models to have a minimum BMI (or meet some appropriate health criteria) to work; and (2) requiring editors and other relevant people to post a disclaimer on images that they digitally altered to make the model look thinner. It does not address, in any detail, the other three limbs of Body Image Law: (3) forbidding altering of images of models' bodies to make them look thinner; (4) requiring retailers to sell clothes in diverse sizes (such a law exists in parts of Argentina);[50] and (5) banning specific words from accompanying the images of models (e.g. 'plus size'). The reason for this is that the research, law and policy in this area currently primarily focuses on the first two limbs of Body Image Law.

The second chapter of this book discusses body image, eating disorders and some of the issues associated with them. It explains four of the main

44 Janet Polivy and C Peter Herman, 'Causes of Eating Disorders' (2002) 53(1) *Annual Review of Psychology* 187, 191 ('Causes of Eating Disorders').

45 Polivy and Herman, 'Causes of Eating Disorders' (n 44) 200; Kristen M Culbert, Sarah E Racine and Kelly L Klump, 'Research Review: What We Have Learned about the Causes of Eating Disorders – a Synthesis of Sociocultural, Psychological, and Biological Research' (2015) 56(11) *Journal of Child Psychology and Psychiatry* 1141, 1157 ('Research Review').

46 Culbert, Racine and Klump, 'Research Review' (n 45) 1157.

47 Polivy and Herman, 'Causes of Eating Disorders' (n 44) 195.

48 Groesz, Levine and Murnen (n 35) 11.

49 Stice et al (n 36) 839.

50 Matt Moffett, 'In Argentine Province, Fashion Police Say Small Isn't Beautiful; Striking Blow for Body Image, Law Seeks Larger Sizes; Eating Yourself Out of Style' (*Wall Street Journal*, Eastern Edition, 26 November 2005, A1).

eating disorders: Anorexia Nervosa, Bulimia Nervosa, Binge Eating Disorder and Avoidant/Restrictive Food Disorder. While there is a myth that eating disorders only impact thin, white women of a high socioeconomic background,[51] this chapter explains the reality that anyone is susceptible to developing one. People from different socioeconomic backgrounds, races, genders and ages can acquire them. It also states some of the costs associated with eating disorders.

The third chapter considers the connection between the thin-ideal and developing poor body image and eating disorders. It also describes two of the main theories that explain why seeing thin-ideal images can result in poor body image and eating disorders for some women: 'Social Comparison Theory' and 'Thin Idealisation'.

The fourth chapter considers social media and body image. It explains some of the studies about how social media can negatively impact body image and the lawsuits known to the author that state that social media contributed to the plaintiff's eating disorder.

The fifth chapter explains what Body Image Law is. It also describes the Body Image Laws that were passed in Israel, France and Norway. It then discusses the body image bills that did not actually become law in the United Kingdom (Federal), Arizona (State), the United States (Federal), Ontario (Provincial) and Brazil (Federal). The chapter describes the bills by dividing them into a few sections: bills that: (a) require models to obtain health certificates to work; (b) ban models below a certain BMI from working on fashion runways; (c) require a government to collect information related to body image; and (d) propose a tax credit for businesses that do not digitally alter images. After this, it examines government and industry policies related to body image: (i) the Quebec Charter for a Healthy and Diverse Body Image (Canada), (ii) the Voluntary Industry Code of Conduct on Body Image (Australia), (iii) Transport for London's Advertising Policy (U.K.), (iv) the Danish Fashion Ethical Charter (Denmark) and (v) the British Fashion Council's Model Health Inquiry (U.K.). It also considers the ban of models below a specific BMI from modelling on runways in Madrid (Spain) and Milan (Italy) and the Council of Fashion Designers of America's (U.S.A.) guidelines concerning models' health. It then explains the self-regulation in the advertising industries that is similar to aspects of Body Image Law that the U.K. Advertising Standards Authority, the Australian Association of

51 S Bryn Austin, 'The Blind Spot in the Drive for Childhood Obesity Prevention: Bringing Eating Disorders Prevention into Focus as a Public Health Priority' (2011) 101(6) *American Journal of Public Health* (1971) e1, e1; Maisie C E Gard and Chris P Freeman, 'The Dismantling of a Myth: A Review of Eating Disorders and Socioeconomic Status' (1996) 20 *International Journal of Eating Disorders* 1, 1; Anne Becker et al, 'Ethnicity and Differential Access to Care for Eating Disorder Symptoms' (2003) 33(2) *The International Journal of Eating Disorders* 205, 206.

National Advertisers and the New Zealand Advertising Standards Authority are responsible for.

Chapter 6 considers challenges with Body Image Law, which fit into two main categories. The first relates to challenges associated with the content of Body Image Law: (1) compelling research found that disclaimers on modified images are ineffective; (2) BMI is an inaccurate measure (the Israeli Body Image Law uses it: models must have a minimum BMI to work and the French Body Image Law takes it into account); (3) Body Image Law does not cover non-commercial images (e.g. images of family, friends and acquaintances), so even in a jurisdiction with a Body Image Law that people abide by, people can still see thin-ideal images of their family, friends, acquaintances, etc.

The second category relates to challenges associated with implementing and enforcing the Law: (1) a 2017 report by the Israeli Knesset identified problems with implementing the Israeli Body Image Law and the difficulty in finding evidence that the Body Image Laws in Israel, France or Norway are being enforced and are effective; (2) there are a significant number of harmful thin-ideal images online; (3) someone who lives in a country with a Body Image Law (even if people abide by it) might still see images of the thin-ideal from another country (which does not have a Body Image Law).

Chapter 7 deals with Pro-Anorexia websites and social media. Pro-Anorexia material promotes Anorexia as a positive lifestyle. This chapter explains what Pro-Anorexia content is and the harm that it can cause. It then explains the law and social media community standards in this area and, in particular, France's bill to address Pro-Anorexia material online: people who posted Pro-Anorexia content online could have faced one year imprisonment and a €10,000 fine if the bill became law and they were found guilty of breaching it.[52] It also considers other potential legislative ways to address preventing Pro-Anorexia content from being online and removing it if it does end up online that differ from the French bill.

Chapter 8 is, arguably, hopeful. This chapter considers what measures might work as part of a successful Body Image Law: one that is most likely to actually result in a positive impact on the body image of people who see thin-ideal images. This chapter does so by considering research in relevant areas, such as psychology. The research falls under two main areas: (1) studies that apply to thin-ideal images: using diverse models, showing unedited images next to edited images, presenting body positive content, not digitally altering images; and (2) studies about measures external to thin-ideal images: rewarding businesses that use models who appear to have healthy bodies and tax initiatives. This chapter briefly explains each of these measures and also which are most feasible from a legal purview.

52 *Loi N° 2016-41 du 26 janvier 2016 de modernisation de notre système de santé* [Law No 2016-41 of 26 January 2016 on the Modernisation of Our Health System] (France).

Chapter 9, the final chapter, summarises this book's key findings and considers the future of body image, eating disorders and Body Image Law. It also briefly discusses how Ozempic affects body image/eating disorders and accordingly, potentially, Body Image Law (arguably no Body Image Law book, published around the year 2025, could be complete without it). It briefly examines how brands use artificial intelligence to create models to use in advertisements (so the images contain non-human models) and how this relates to Body Image Law (arguably no Body Image Law book published around the year 2025 could be complete without discussing this issue, either). This book tries to end on a message of optimism and hopeful hashtags.

This book also contains five standalone tables as annexures: Annexure A lists all the Body Image Laws in the world, including laws, bills and policy, organised by jurisdiction, known to the author. Annexure B lists all of the rulings by advertising self-regulators in Australia, the United Kingdom and New Zealand found by the author concerning advertisements that a person complained to the relevant regulator had an issue that was negatively related to body image. Annexure C lists the community standards that different social media have that discuss Pro-Anorexia content. Annexure D states the Body Image Law-related topics that the author recommends could benefit from further research that are otherwise scattered throughout this book. Annexure E is a list of all the scholarly work that the author could find which she believes is primarily about Body Image Law or assesses the impact of implementing Body Image Law or similar policies. The Annexures in this book are chiefly meant to aid other researchers in this area, including higher degrees by research students, and to encourage further research in this relatively new, important and fascinating legal area. Annexure E, in particular, also tries to help establish Body Image Law as its own discrete legal area.

This book also provides valuable analysis and refers to many peer-reviewed publications from psychology, public health and other relevant disciplines. The author tried to write this book so that no matter your discipline, be it law, psychology, public health, political science, etc., or none thereof, you should be able to understand it.

This book takes an international perspective: it examines body image, eating disorders and Body Image Law in many areas around the world, including Australia, Canada, Brazil, the United Kingdom, the United States and France. The available research on this topic is primarily from developed countries, so this book concentrates on material from those areas.

If there is one thing that the author hopes that this book accomplishes for you (and it is unrelated to law) it is this: to make you contemplate (if you have not already) that the thin-ideal is an artificial concept that you should not try to aspire to, nor should you expect anyone else to.

There is a second thing that the author hopes that this book accomplishes for you, also unrelated to law. When you see the thin-ideal or any type of appearance that is presented as ideal and aspirational, instead of comparing yourself to it, and/or trying to achieve it, try to challenge what you see and any negative feelings that you may experience from seeing it. For example, upon seeing an image of the thin-ideal, you might think: who is profiting if I feel bad about my body because it does not look like the thin-ideal? (The answer might be advertisers and companies trying to sell weight loss products, among others.) You might also think: what useful things can I do for myself, or my loved ones, with the time that I currently spend feeling bad about my body, or trying to change it to adhere to an artificial, narrow version of beauty that will likely change in the future? The author hopes that this book accomplishes even more for you, which will be revealed in due course.

2 Body Image and Eating Disorders Generally and Associated Socioeconomic Issues

Introduction

> Body image is defined as one's perception, thoughts, and emotions revolving around one's own body. It is the depiction of one's body representation, including their mirror reflection, and it reflects social constructs, which depend on a society's culture and norms. This conception is created using body ideals, substantially communicated via media, family, and peers.[1]

As well, body image 'is a multidimensional construct, including emotions, cognitions, and behaviors related to appearance'.[2] Women who have good body image are more likely to be mentally and physically healthy.[3]

About 9% of Americans, approximately 29 million people, will develop an eating disorder sometime in their life.[4] About 1.25 million British people have eating disorders,[5] approximately 1.1 million Australians have an eating disorder,[6] between 30,000 and 40,000 people in France have Anorexia Nervosa[7] and between 725,800 and 1,088,700 Canadians have an eating

1 Barbara Jiotsa et al, 'Social Media Use and Body Image Disorders: Association between Frequency of Comparing One's Own Physical Appearance to That of People Being Followed on Social Media and Body Dissatisfaction and Drive for Thinness' (2021) 18(6) *International Journal of Environmental Research and Public Heath* 2880, 2880.

2 Rachel F Rodgers, Susan J Paxton and Eleanor H Wertheim, 'Take Idealized Bodies out of the Picture: A Scoping Review of Social Media Content Aiming to Protect and Promote Positive Body Image' (2021) 38 *Body Image* 10, 24.

3 Office on Women's Health, 'Body Image' (Web Page, 3 February 2025) <https://womenshealth.gov/mental-health/body-image-and-mental-health/body-image>.

4 National Association of Anorexia Nervosa and Associated Disorders, 'Eating Disorder Statistics' (Web Page, 29 November 2023) <https://anad.org/eating-disorder-statistic/>.

5 Danielle Gash, 'The Many Faces of Eating Disorders' (2024) 403(10440) *The Lancet (British edition)* 1976, 1976.

6 Deloitte, *The Economic and Social Impact of Eating Disorders in Australia: Paying the Price* (Butterfly Foundation, 2nd ed, 2024) 9 <https://butterfly.org.au/wp-content/uploads/2024/10/deloitte-au-eco-paying-the-price-second-edition-180724-new-Oct-24.pdf> ('Paying the Price').

7 Alissa J Rubin, 'French Parliament Debates Weight Standards for Fashion Models', *The New York Times* (online, 18 March 2015) <https://www.nytimes.com/2015/03/19/world/europe/french-parliament-debates-weight-standards-for-fashion-models.html>.

DOI: 10.4324/9781003678793-2

disorder.[8] In community-based studies, the estimates of the 'combined lifetime prevalence of all DSM-5 eating disorders among adolescent and young adult women ranged from 5.5 to 17.9%'.[9]

Four of the main eating disorders are Anorexia Nervosa, Bulimia Nervosa, Binge Eating Disorder and Avoidant/Restrictive Food Intake Disorder. This chapter will briefly describe each, as well as disordered eating. After this, it will explain the research about eating disorders and socioeconomic status, race/ethnicity and gender. It will also succinctly examine the cost of eating disorders.

The Four Main Eating Disorders and Avoidant/Restrictive Food Intake Disorder

Anorexia Nervosa involves eating insufficient amounts of food, which results in having a very low body weight, and being afraid of gaining weight or having a larger body and shape is very significant to the person who has it.[10] Anorexia Nervosa can damage the brain, and even if a person who has it recovers, the damage to their brain might not reverse fully.[11] A person with Anorexia Nervosa resists treatment and has a high risk of dying from complications from their illness.[12] Also, it is important to mention Atypical Anorexia Nervosa: a person who has this illness satisfies all of the criteria for Anorexia Nervosa; however, even though they lost weight, their weight is still considered average, or above average.[13]

A person who has Bulimia Nervosa eats significant amounts of food regularly and then purges.[14] They purge through, for example, fasting,

8 Ontario Community Outreach Program for Eating Disorders and National Initiative for Eating Disorders, 'Canadian Research on Eating Disorders' (Online) <https://nedic.ca/download-file/1540817045.365148-41/&ved=2ahUKEwj2vaSZ4M-MAxWYzjgGHdrKEIMQFnoECBEQAQ&usg=AOvVaw2mrpsn400KtpqpXEC10dLw>.

9 Yasmina Silen and Anna Keski-Rahkonen, 'Worldwide Prevalence of DSM-5 Eating Disorders Among Young People' (2022) *Current Opinions Psychiatry* 362–364.

10 American Psychiatric Association (ed), *Diagnostic and Statistical Manual of Mental Disorders: DSM-5-TR* (American Psychiatric Association Publishing, 5th ed, 2022) ('DSM-5').

11 Sophie Scharner and Andreas Stengel, 'Alterations of Brain Structure and Functions in Anorexia Nervosa' (2019) 28 *Clinical Nutrition Experimental* 22, 29, 30.

12 James E Mitchell, Carol B Peterson and Caren G Solomon, 'Anorexia Nervosa' (2020) 382(14) *The New England Journal of Medicine* 1343-1351, 1343.

13 American Psychiatric Association, DSM-5 (n 10).

14 Emre Bora and Sezen Kose, 'Meta-Analysis of Theory of Mind in Anorexia Nervosa and Bulimia Nervosa: A Specific Impairment of Cognitive Perspective Taking in Anorexia Nervosa?' (2016) 49(8) *The International Journal of Eating Disorders* 739, 740; American Psychiatric Association, DSM-5 (n 10).

overexercising or vomiting.[15] The bingeing and purging must occur weekly for at least three months to fit the criteria for this illness. It is associated with self-harm and dying.[16] People with Bulimia Nervosa think about their body shape and weight frequently. They typically have a normal or above normal weight.[17]

Binge Eating Disorder involves eating significant amounts of food regularly, but unlike Bulimia Nervosa, the person who has it does not purge[18] and feels like they cannot control their eating.[19] People with Binge Eating Disorder may obsessively think about food, be worried about their weight and have low mood,[20] eat quickly, until they are very full and feel out of control.[21] It is the most diagnosed eating disorder.[22]

Avoidant/Restrictive Food Intake Disorder involves 'an eating or feeding disturbance' (for example, not being interested in food, avoiding food due to sensory features, not liking the consequences of eating) and is associated with one or more of these: (1) significant weight loss, (2) being notably nutritionally deficient, (3) using a feeding tube or nutritional supplements, (4) illness interfering with their ability to undertake daily tasks.[23]

A person who has disordered eating tries to become thin or remain thin, but does not fit the requirements to have an eating disorder, like Anorexia Nervosa or Bulimia Nervosa.[24] They may restrict their calories, exercise compulsively, binge and purge and use laxatives.[25] Potential 'risk factors' for developing disordered eating include social-cultural factors (such as the media's influence) and personality attributes (likely perfectionism and neuroticism).[26]

15 American Psychiatric Association, DSM-5 (n 10); Tracey D Wade, 'Recent Research on Bulimia Nervosa' (2019) 42 *Psychiatric Clinics of North America* 21, 21.
16 Tracey D Wade, 'Recent Research on Bulimia Nervosa' (2019) 42 *Psychiatric Clinics of North America* 21, 24.
17 American Psychiatric Association, DSM-5 (n 10).
18 Cynthia M Bulik et al, 'The Changing "Weightscape" of Bulimia Nervosa' (2012) 169(10) *The American Journal of Psychiatry* 1031, 1031.
19 American Psychiatric Association, DSM-5 (n 10).
20 Kimberly A Brownley et al, 'Binge-Eating Disorder in Adults: A Systematic Review and Meta-Analysis' (2016) 165(6) *Annals of Internal Medicine* 409, 414.
21 Anja Hilbert, 'Binge-Eating Disorder' (2018) 42(1) *The Psychiatric Clinics of North America* 33, 33.
22 Bing Feng et al, 'Current Discoveries and Future Implications of Eating Disorders' (2023) 20(14) *International Journal of Environmental Research and Public Health* 1, 6.
23 American Psychiatric Association, DSM-5 (n 10).
24 Sharlene Hesse-Biber et al, 'The Mass Marketing of Disordered Eating and Eating Disorders: The Social Psychology of Women, Thinness and Culture' (2006) 29 *Women's Studies International Forum* 208, 211.
25 Ibid.
26 Kristen M Culbert, Sarah E Racine and Kelly L Klump, 'Research Review: What We Have Learned about the Causes of Eating Disorders – a Synthesis of Sociocultural, Psychological, and Biological Research' (2015) 56(11) *Journal of Child Psychology and Psychiatry* 1141, 1157.

The research on body image and eating disorders also uses the term 'body dissatisfaction', which is 'a person's negative thoughts and feelings about his or her body'.[27] A person who has body dissatisfaction may later develop an eating disorder.[28]

If someone who has an eating disorder does not seek treatment, this can reduce the length of their life.[29] They may also experience challenges to their relationships and economic problems.[30] Discussing having an eating disorder can be taboo for some and might cause the person who has an eating disorder to be stigmatised.[31] The stereotypes that people have about eating disorders, such as from the media, can also prevent the people who have them from seeking treatment.[32] Other reasons why people may not receive treatment for their eating disorder include: clinicians not perceiving that certain people need such treatment (for example, people who are racial or ethnic minorities) and not having treatment resources for certain people (for example, people who have Binge Eating Disorder or men).[33]

It is important to know which demographic groups have eating disorders to distribute the resources necessary to treat them.[34] There is an abundance of evidence which dispels the myth that only white, rich women in developed countries have eating disorders,[35] which this chapter will explain briefly. Specially, it will examine eating disorders and socioeconomic status, race/ethnicity and gender.

27 Sarah Grogan, *Body Image Understanding Body Dissatisfaction in Men, Women and Children* (Taylor and Francis, 2nd ed., 2007) 4.

28 P Rohde, E Stice and CN Marti, 'Development and Predictive Effects of Eating Disorder Risk Factors During Adolescence: Implications for Prevention Efforts' (2015) 48(2) *International Journal of Eating Disorders* 1, 9.

29 Britney Clasper, 'Conceptualising a Preventative Approach to Eating Disorders in New Zealand' [2023] *New Zealand Law Students' Journal* 105, 110.

30 Ibid 108.

31 Ibid 158.

32 Rachel Baffsky, 'Eating Disorders in Australia: A Commentary on the Need to Address Stigma' (2020) 8(1) *Journal of Eating Disorders* 1, 1–2.

33 KR Sonneville and SK Lipson, 'Disparities in Eating Disorder Diagnosis and Treatment According to Weight Status, Race/Ethnicity, Socioeconomic Background, and Sex among College Students' (2018) 51(6) *The International Journal of Eating Disorders* 518, 519.

34 Natasha L Burke et al, 'Socioeconomic Status and Eating Disorder Prevalence: At the Intersections of Gender Identity, Sexual Orientation, and Race/Ethnicity' (2023) 53(9) *Psychological Medicine* 4255, 4255.

35 S Bryn Austin, 'The Blind Spot in the Drive for Childhood Obesity Prevention: Bringing Eating Disorders Prevention into Focus as a Public Health Priority' (2011) 101(6) *American Journal of Public Health* (1971) e1, e1; Maisie C E Gard and Chris P Freeman, 'The Dismantling of a Myth: A Review of Eating Disorders and Socioeconomic Status' (1996) 20 *International Journal of Eating Disorders* 1, 1 ('The Dismantling of a Myth'); Anne Becker et al, 'Ethnicity and Differential Access to Care for Eating Disorder Symptoms' (2003) 33(2) *The International Journal of Eating Disorders* 205, 206.

Eating Disorders and Socioeconomic Status

The idea that a significant number of people who have eating disorders are in high socioeconomic groups appears to be based primarily on small numbers of cases of Anorexia Nervosa from clinical samples, including many tertiary referrals.[36] Until the early 1980s, all the studies involving eating disorders that considered socioeconomic status only examined Anorexia Nervosa.[37] Due to the stereotype that eating disorders mainly affect young women from higher socioeconomic backgrounds,[38] eating disorder treatment focused on this demographic.[39] It is possible that, consequently, when people who are from lower socioeconomic backgrounds have eating disorders, clinicians fail to diagnose them.[40]

There is persuasive research that eating disorders are prevalent among all socioeconomic backgrounds. A systemic review of the literature on Anorexia Nervosa, Bulimia Nervosa and Binge Eating Disorder found evidence which does not substantiate the idea that primarily people of a higher socioeconomic background experience these illnesses.[41]

An Australian study using information from South Australian surveys that involved face-to-face interviews of 5,000 households[42] found that eating disorder rates were similar across different levels of household income and various socioeconomic status indicators.[43]

Eating Disorders and Race and Ethnicity

Race and ethnicity intersect with eating disorders.[44] Race and ethnicity may appear to 'overlap'.[45] The terms can be challenging to define and it is contentious how and whether to collect this information.[46]

36 Gard and Freeman, 'The Dismantling of a Myth' (n 35) 5.

37 Ibid 8.

38 Ibid 1.

39 Brittany Mulders-Jones et al, 'Socioeconomic Correlates of Eating Disorder Symptoms in an Australian Population-Based Sample' (2017) 12(1) *PLOS One* 1, 2.

40 Kathryn M Huryk, Catherine R Drury and Katharine L Loeb, 'Diseases of Affluence? A Systematic Review of the Literature on Socioeconomic Diversity in Eating Disorders' (2021) 43 *Eating Behaviors: An International Journal* 1, 2.

41 Ibid 13.

42 Mulders-Jones (Ibid 39) 5.

43 Ibid 9.

44 See, for example, B Dolan, JH Lacey and C Evans, 'Eating Behaviour and Attitudes to Weight and Shape in British Women from Three Ethnic Groups' (1990) 157 *British Journal of Psychiatry* 523.

45 Amy H Egbert et al, 'Reporting Racial and Ethnic Diversity in Eating Disorder Research over the Past 20 Years' (2022) 55(4) *The International Journal of Eating Disorders* 455, 456.

46 Ibid.

Race is 'the social construction and categorisation of people based on perceived shared physical traits that result in the maintenance of a sociopolitical hierarchy. The term is also loosely applied to geographic, cultural, religious, or national groups.'[47] Ethnicity is 'a characterization of people based on having a shared culture (e.g., language, food, music, dress, values, and beliefs) related to common ancestry and shared history'.[48] Understanding how ethnicity and race intersect with eating disorders is important to preventing eating disorders.[49]

It has been found that white people are more likely to be diagnosed with and treated for an eating disorder than people of other races or ethnicities,[50] even though people in all ethnic and racial groups can have eating disorders[51] and there is no major difference in eating disorder prevalence among different ethnic groups.[52]

Similarly, it has been found that clinicians are less likely to refer people who are part of an ethnic minority for eating disorder treatment, even though people who are an ethnic minority and those who are not may have similar symptoms.[53] Doctors also tend to ask people who are an ethnic minority less about their eating disorder symptoms than those who are not.[54]

Eating Disorders and Men

There is little eating disorder research that solely involves men;[55] most is about women.[56] It is easier to identify and research weight loss than changing

47 *APA Dictionary of Psychology* (online at 11 April 2025) 'race' <https://dictionary.apa.org/race>.
48 Ibid.
49 Melissa Simone et al, 'Ethnic/Racial and Gender Differences in Disordered Eating Behavior Prevalence Trajectories among Women and Men from Adolescence into Adulthood' (2022) 294 *Social Science & Medicine* 1, 2.
50 Sonneville and Lipson (n 33) 519–522.
51 Tomoko Udo and Carlos M Grilo, 'Prevalence and Correlates of DSM-5–Defined Eating Disorders in a Nationally Representative Sample of U.S. Adults' (2018) 84(5) *Biological Psychiatry* (1969) 345, 352.
52 Zhen Hadassah Chenga et al, 'Ethnic Differences in Eating Disorder Prevalence, Risk Factors, and Predictive Effects of Risk Factors among Young Women' (2019) 32 *Eating Behaviours* 23, 27.
53 Anne Becker et al, 'Ethnicity and Differential Access to Care for Eating Disorder Symptoms' (2003) 33(2) *The International Journal of Eating Disorders* 205, 210–211.
54 Ibid.
55 Sasha Gorrell and Stuart B Murray, 'Eating Disorders in Males' (2019) 28(4) *Child and Adolescent Psychiatric Clinics of North America* 641, 642 ('Eating Disorders in Males').
56 Christopher P Barlett, Christopher L Vowels and Donald A Saucier, 'Meta-Analyses of the Effects of Media Images on Men's Body-Image Concerns' (2008) 27(3) *Journal of Social and Clinical Psychology* 279, 281.

muscle size, which can result in a gender bias in eating disorder research.[57] While women are more likely to be diagnosed with an eating disorder than men,[58] it is becoming more common that men have eating disorders,[59] and there is increasing pressure on them to have an ideal body.[60]

It is probable that men are preoccupied with being muscular than their weight being a certain number, whereas women are likely to be more concerned with losing weight.[61] Further, while women may seek to match the thin-ideal, men might strive for an ideal body with low amounts of body fat and a 'v' shape: broad shoulders, a narrow waist and a muscular chest and upper arms.[62] Some men experience Muscle Dysmorphia: they are strict about their eating, weight train compulsively and are concerned about their body shape and weight.[63]

Eating disorders in men are underdiagnosed:[64] many people wrongly believe that men do not experience them.[65] Resources for treating eating disorders for men are limited: they are primarily aimed at women.[66] Men often do not mention their eating disorders and they may feel shame for having them.[67]

Researchers also found that when some men see images of men in the mass media with the ideal body it can result in negative body image.[68] They discovered that the effect was worse on study participants who were in college than in high school.[69] Seeing images of the ideal male body can also make some men feel dissatisfied with their muscles and increase depression.[70] When some boys read health and fitness magazines, this can result in them deciding to take pills and supplements to try to become more muscular.[71] Even holding muscular male action figures can result in some men having poor body

57 John F Morgan, 'From Charles Atlas to Adonis Complex—Fat Is More than a Feminist Issue' (2000) 356(9239) *The Lancet (British edition)* 1372, 1373.

58 See Udo and Grilo (n 51) 352.

59 Georg Halbeisen et al, 'Eating Disorders in Men' (2024) 121(3) *Deutsches Ärzteblatt International* 86, 90.

60 Renée A Botta, 'For Your Health? The Relationship between Magazine Reading and Adolescents' Body Image and Eating Disturbances' (2003) 48(9–10) *Sex Roles* 389, 390.

61 Morgan (n 57) 1373.

62 Halbeisen et al (n 59) 88; Gorrell and Murray (n 53) 642.

63 Roland Müller, 'Muscle Dysmorphia: Appearance, Diagnostic Approaches, Research and Treatment' *EC* (2020) 9.3 *Psychology and Psychiatry* 1, 2.

64 Eric Strother et al, 'Eating Disorders in Men: Underdiagnosed, Undertreated, and Misunderstood' (2012) 20(5) *Eating Disorders* 346, 347; Gorrell and Murray (n 53) 642.

65 Allison A Vaughan and Joshua D Lowe, 'With Age Comes Responsibility: Changes in Stigma for Boys/Men with Bulimia Nervosa' (2020) 25(6) *Eating and Weight Disorders* 1525, 1525.

66 Strother et al (n 64) 346.

67 Halbeisen et al (n 529) 89.

68 Barlett, Vowels and Saucier (n 56) 301.

69 Ibid 302–303.

70 Daniel Agliata and Stacey Tantleff-Dunn, 'The Impact of Media Exposure on Males' Body Image' (2004) 23(1) *Journal of Social and Clinical Psychology* 7, 16.

71 Botta (n 60) 396.

esteem.[72] When men see images of attractive and muscular shirtless men on Instagram, it can lower their body satisfaction.[73]

The author notes that the Body Image Law that is the raison d'être of this book is aimed at creating change regarding women's poor body image and their experiencing eating disorders, not men, even though boys and men also suffer from poor body image and eating disorders. Laws involving men's body image might focus on disclaimers that state that men in advertisements used steroids or other illegal performance enhancements for muscular enhancement or make it illegal for advertisers to use male models who used steroids or other illegal performance enhancements.[74] A complexity involved with this issue is the illegality of taking steroids in many jurisdictions could make men reluctant to admit that they took them for fear of being charged with a criminal offence.[75] Law involving men's body image could also involve forbidding digitally altering images of men to make them look more muscular or that require disclaimers that state that men's bodies were edited to make them look more muscular or that require advertisers to use male models with diverse body types.

Analysing these topics are outside the purview of the author's expertise but research and dialogue about them are important on a macro level to try to reduce the number of men who suffer from poor body image and eating disorders. The author is unaware of any Body Image Law in the world that specifically deals with the impact of males seeing images of men with the ideal male body. Nevertheless, the author considers it important to acknowledge that body image and eating disorders in the male context is a very important issue and this book does not discuss it in depth only because it is outside her expertise.

The Cost of Eating Disorders

Eating disorders can result in significant health care costs and lowered tax revenue due to decreased productivity.[76] In the United States, the total financial cost of eating disorders for 2018–2019 was estimated to be $64.7 billion

72 Chris Barlett et al, 'Action Figures and Men' (2005) 53(11–12) *Sex Roles* 877, 884.
73 Marika Tiggemann and Isabella Anderberg, 'Muscles and Bare Chests on Instagram: The Effect of Influencers' Fashion and Fitspiration Images on Men's Body Image' (2020) 35 *Body Image* 237, 241.
74 See, for example, Marilyn Bromberg and Tomas Fitzgerald, 'Male Body Image Issues Shows Men Chase Impossible Ideals' *The West Australian* (online, 20 March 2024) <https://thewest.com.au/opinion/male-body-image-issues-shows-men-chase-impossible-ideals-c-14006763>.
75 Ibid.
76 Deloitte, Paying the Price (n 6) 23.

(U.S.), or $11,808 per person who had an eating disorder.[77] Health system costs were 7.0% of the total, which was $4.6 billion.[78] From this, Americans paid $363.5 million in out-of-pocket costs towards their eating disorder.[79] In Australia, approximately 1.1 million people or about 4.45% of the population have an eating disorder and people aged 15–19 are most likely to have one.[80] The total 'economic and social cost' of eating disorders in Australia was $66.9 billion in 2023, which equals $60,654 per person with an eating disorder.[81] The financial costs associated with eating disorders in Australia in 2023 was $20.8 billion.[82] The total health costs related to eating disorders in Australia were estimated to be about $251.4 million in 2023. These costs include prescription medicine, expenditures on being admitted as a patient in hospital and visits to psychologists and general practitioners.[83] The annual cost of eating disorders in the United Kingdom to the National Health Service is between £3.9 billion and £4.6 billion.[84]

Conclusion

This chapter of the book briefly summarised the main eating disorders and Avoidant/Restrictive Food Intake Disorder. These illnesses are serious, tragic and affect many people worldwide. This chapter also addressed the myth that eating disorders only affect white women who have a high socioeconomic status. Anyone, no matter their socioeconomic status, race, ethnicity, gender, etc., can have an eating disorder.

77 Deloitte Access Economics, 'Social and Economic Cost of Eating Disorders in the US' (June 2020) <https://www.deloitte.com/au/en/services/economics/perspectives/social-economic-cost-eating-disorders-united-states.html>.

78 Ibid.

79 Ibid.

80 Deloitte, Paying the Price (n 6) 27.

81 Ibid 11.

82 Ibid 32.

83 Ibid 34.

84 Beating Eating Disorders, *The Cost of Eating Disorders* <https://beat.contentfiles.net/media/documents/The_costs_of_eating_disorders_2015.pdf> 9.

3 Theories to Explain the Connection between Seeing Images of the Thin-Ideal and Developing Poor Body Image and Eating Disorders

Introduction

The mass media influences values, norms and aesthetic ideals.[1] Beauty and fashion advertisements frequently portray an unrealistic view of what women look like, which has led to growing concern about how advertisements can impact body image and self-esteem.[2] Seeing thin-ideal images can cause lowered mood[3] and is associated with lowered body satisfaction and symptoms of Anorexia Nervosa and Bulimia Nervosa.[4]

Body Image Law is concerned with the connection, for some people, between seeing thin-ideal images and the harm that can result from it. This chapter will consider the theories that explain this connection.

Social Comparison Theory

Social Comparison Theory can explain why it can be harmful to women when they see thin-ideal images.[5] This theory was first discussed in 1954 and has been applied often ever since.[6] Social Comparison Theory states that people

1 K Harrison and J Cantor, 'The Relationship Between Media Consumption and Eating Disorders' (1997) 47(1) *Journal of Communication* 40, 41.

2 Ashley O'Neil, 'A Call for Truth in the Fashion Pages: What Global Trend in Advertising Regulation Means for U.S. Beauty and Fashion Advertisers' (2014) 21(2) *Indiana Journal of Global Legal Studies* 619, 620.

3 Rachel Cohen et al, '#BoPo on Instagram: An Experimental Investigation of the Effects of Viewing Body Positive Content on Young Women's Mood and Body Image' (2019) 21(7) *New Media & Society* 1546, 1558.

4 Shelly Grabe, Monique L Ward and Janet Shibley, 'The Role of the Media in Body Image Concerns among Women: A Meta-Analysis of Experimental and Correlational Studies' (2008) 134(3) *Psychological Bulletin* 460, 470.

5 Taryn A Myers, Janis H Crowther and David Watson, 'Social Comparison as a Predictor of Body Dissatisfaction: A Meta-Analytic Review' (2009) 118(4) *Journal of Abnormal Psychology* 683, 691.

6 Ferhat Caliskan et al, 'Social Comparison Theory: A Review and Future Directions' (2024) 41(11) *Psychology & Marketing* 2823, 2823.

DOI: 10.4324/9781003678793-3

often compare themselves to others to evaluate themselves.[7] People who want to improve on a particular attribute compare themselves with someone who is better in that attribute (upward comparison) which can have negative results, such as lower self-esteem.[8] When people compare themselves with others who they feel are not as good as themselves (downward comparison) this is likely to have positive results, such as better self-esteem.[9] For some women, downward social comparisons can be good for their body image and upward social comparisons can harm it.[10] Comparing one's body to others is also related to higher levels of body dissatisfaction.[11] Additionally, researchers found that most appearance comparisons made through social and traditional media were upward and negatively impacted women's appearance satisfaction.[12] The upward comparisons through social media had a worse impact on women's mood than traditional media.[13] Specific social media features, such as users liking or commenting on photographs, may result in upward comparisons on social media having more of an impact than when people compare themselves to others in person.[14] This book will discuss social media and body image in the next chapter.

Thin-Ideal Internalisation

Another explanation for why seeing images of thin-ideal women can harm the body image of some women is internalising the beauty ideal or thin internalisation:[15] how much a woman seeks to conform to what society believes is attractive.[16] While most people know about society's beauty

7 Leon Festinger, 'A Theory of Social Comparison Processes' (1954) 7(2) *Human Relations (New York)* 117, 117–138.

8 Ibid.

9 Ibid.

10 Silvia Moreno-Dominguez et al, 'Images of Thin and Plus-Size Models Produce Opposite Effects on Women's Body Image, Body Dissatisfaction, and Anxiety' (2019) 80(9–10) *Sex Roles* 607, 612.

11 Myers, Crowther and Watson (n 5) 691.

12 Jasmine Fardouly, Rebecca T Pinkus and Lenny R Vartanian, 'The Impact of Appearance Comparisons Made through Social Media, Traditional Media, and in Person in Women's Everyday Lives' (2017) 20 *Body Image* 31, 38.

13 Ibid.

14 Ibid 36.

15 Kevin J Thompson and Leslie J Heinberg, 'The Media's Influence on Body Image Disturbance and Eating Disorders: We've Reviled Them, Now Can We Rehabilitate Them?' (1999) 55(2) *Journal of Social Issues* 339, 350.

16 Kevin J Thompson, *Exacting Beauty: Theory, Assessment, and Treatment of Body Image Disturbance* (American Psychological Association, 1999) 98–99.

standards, not everyone supports them. People who do have a greater risk of having an eating disorder or body dissatisfaction.[17]

A Real-Life Example of How Seeing Images of the Thin-Ideal Can Impact Body Image and Eating Disorders: Fiji

The spread of eating disorders in Fiji, an archipelago with over 300 islands, near Melanesia and Polynesia, provides a helpful example to demonstrate the impact that seeing thin-ideal images can have.[18] Before the mid-1990s, very few people in Fiji had eating disorders: only a single person was known to have Anorexia Nervosa.[19] Fijians were not interested in reshaping their bodies.[20] In 1995, Western television was introduced in Fiji for the first time.[21] This was associated with a major increase in the prevalence of women having disordered eating indicators.[22] For example, in 1995, the year that Western television was introduced in Fiji, none of the ethnic Fijian adolescents enrolled in two secondary schools in the study reported using self-induced vomiting to affect their weight, but three years later 11.3% of the study participants reported that they had.[23]

Conclusion

This brief chapter addressed the connection between seeing thin-ideal images and some women developing poor body image and eating disorders. This connection is key to Body Image Law: because ideally, Body Image Law should be a metaphorical hammer that helps to smash this connection into non-existence.

17 Sarah Barakat et al, 'Risk Factors for Eating Disorders: Findings from a Rapid Review' (2023) 11(1) *Journal of Eating Disorders* 8, 19.

18 Anne E Becker, 'Television, Disordered Eating, and Young Women in Fiji: Negotiating Body Image and Identity During Rapid Social Change' (2004)28(4) *Culture, Medicine and Psychiatry* 553, 538 ('Television, Disordered Eating').

19 Anne E Becker et al, 'Eating Behaviours and Attitudes Following Prolonged Exposure to Television among Ethnic Fijian Adolescent Girls' (2002) 180(6) *British Journal of Psychiatry* 509, 509 ('Eating Behaviours').

20 Becker, 'Television, Disordered Eating' (n 19) 538–539.

21 Ibid 558.

22 Becker et al, 'Eating Behaviours' (n 20) 511.

23 Ibid 509–510.

4 How Social Media Impacts Body Image

Introduction

> The term 'social media' refers to every website and online mobile app with user-generated content. They enable their users to participate in online exchanges, broadcast self-made content, and join virtual communities. They are mostly used by teenagers and young adults, and the most common ones are Facebook, Instagram, Snapchat, and Twitter.[1]

Moreover, the 'evolution of social media has been fueled by the human impulse to communicate and by advances in digital technology. It is a story about establishing and nurturing personal connections at scale'.[2] Social media material differs from traditional media content because peers and influencers create a lot of it and it is interactive.[3]

Instagram has more than 1 billion users worldwide,[4] Facebook has approximately 1.7 billion users worldwide,[5] Reddit has about 300 million users worldwide[6] and TikTok has more than 800 million users worldwide.[7] Social media is unique because it has countless images that are 'carefully curated'.[8]

1 Barbara Jiotsa et al, 'Social Media Use and Body Image Disorders: Association between Frequency of Comparing One's Own Physical Appearance to That of People Being Followed on Social Media and Body Dissatisfaction and Drive for Thinness' (2021) 18(6) *International Journal of Environmental Research and Public Heath* 1, 2.

2 'The Evolution of Social Media: How Did It Begin, and Where Could It Go Next?', *Maryville University Online* (28 May 2020) <https://online.maryville.edu/blog/evolution-social-media/> ('The Evolution').

3 Marika Tiggemann and Isabella Anderberg, 'Social Media is not Real: The Effect of 'Instagram vs Reality' Images on Women's Social Comparison and Body Image' (2020) 22(12) *New Media & Society* 2183, 2184.

4 'The Evolution' (n 2).

5 Ibid.

6 Ibid.

7 Ibid.

8 Rachel Cohen et al, '#BoPo on Instagram: An Experimental Investigation of the Effects of Viewing Body Positive Content on Young Women's Mood and Body Image' (2019) 21(7) *New Media & Society* 1546, 1547.

DOI: 10.4324/9781003678793-4

The author will not further explain what social media is. Many explanations are available elsewhere, including some by the author,[9] and…it's 2025.

Thin-ideal images are ubiquitous on social media.[10] When you join social media, you see terms and conditions. Even if you read every word, nowhere will you see that when you use it you may see countless numbers of these thin-ideal images, which are usually of people also looking their very best and frequently digitally altered. Nor do they warn you about the psychological harm that seeing these images can cause some people. This chapter does. It also describes some of the lawsuits that plaintiffs commenced against social media which alleged that social media use contributed to their eating disorder.

Research Relating to How Social Media Can Negatively Impact Body Image

> A decade or so ago, it seemed highly reasonable to think that social media might be very beneficial for body image (e.g. Andsager, 2014). Finally, women and girls (and men and boys) would no longer be exposed to and compare themselves with all those beautiful models in the magazines, but instead, would now be exposed to the diverse range of normal body sizes and shapes exhibited by their peers, i.e. ordinary people…But it hasn't turned out that way...So what went wrong? First, although the content of social media is largely peer-generated, social media are also used by celebrities, models, Influencers, fitness gurus, and other beautiful people who adhere to idealized beauty standards to promote themselves and their products. Such accounts can have millions of followers and a large presence on social media. Second, otherwise average-looking people post a curated highlight reel of only their best photos, ones in which they look good or are doing something noteworthy. In particular, many women and girls report spending considerable time and effort in taking and selecting the photo to be uploaded…As a consequence, although it consists largely of peers who come in a range of shapes and sizes, the social media environment presents unrealistic and idealized images for women and girls (and men and boys).[11]

9 See, for example, Marilyn Bromberg-Krawitz, 'Issues Paper for a Symposium: Challenges of Social Media for Courts & Tribunals' (Paper for the Australasian Institute of Judicial Administration Incorporated and the Judicial Conference of Australia, May 2016) 2–6 <https://aija.org.au/wp-content/uploads/2017/07/Krawitz.pdf>.

10 Pilar Aparicio-Martinez et al, 'Social Media, Thin-Ideal, Body Dissatisfaction and Disordered Eating Attitudes: An Exploratory Analysis' (2019) 16(21) *International Journal of Environmental Research and Public Health* 1, 12.

11 Marika Tiggemann, 'Digital Modification and Body Image on Social Media: Disclaimer Labels, Captions, Hashtags, and Comments' (2022) 41 *Body Image* 172, 173.

Meta-analysis supports the idea that seeing the thin-ideal on social media 'has a causal, negative impact on body image'.[12] Further, comparing your body to other people's bodies that you see on social media 'is associated with' poorer body image.[13]

Social media, like traditional media, has a very high number of thin-ideal images.[14] Users typically post content that relates to appearance and comment on others' appearance-related posts, which could influence how people feel about their appearance.[15] There is 'an association between the frequency of comparing one's own physical appearance to that of people followed on social media and body dissatisfaction and drive for thinness'.[16]

Visual social media, like Instagram, are more harmful to body image than those that are less visual, like Facebook.[17] A study by *Wall Street Journal* staff from around 2020 found that when girls already felt poorly about their bodies, spending time on Instagram made them feel worse.[18] Around this time, researchers from Instagram learned that using Instagram worsens body image for one in three teenage girls.[19] Women who spend more time on Facebook may compare their appearance to others on Facebook to a greater extent and be further concerned about their body.[20] Women compare themselves most to distant peers and least to family members on social media.[21]

Well-known Meta whistleblower Frances Haugen said that Meta's 'leadership knows ways to make Facebook and Instagram safer and won't make the necessary changes because they have put their immense profits before

12 Madelaine K de Valle et al, 'Social Media, Body Image, and the Question of Causation: Meta-Analyses of Experimental and Longitudinal Evidence' (2021) *Body Image* 276, 285.

13 Rubinia Celeste Bonfanti et al, 'The Association between Social Comparison in Social Media, Body Image Concerns and Eating Disorder Symptoms: A Systematic Review and Meta-Analysis' (2025) 52 *Body Image* 1, 7.

14 Cohen et al (n 8) 1547.

15 Jasmine Fardouly and Lenny R Vartanian, 'Social Media and Body Image Concerns: Current Research and Future Directions' (2016) 9 *Current Opinion in Psychology* 1, 1.

16 Jiotsa et al (n 1) 12.

17 Renee Engeln et al, 'Compared to Facebook, Instagram Use Causes More Appearance Comparison and Lower Body Satisfaction in College Women' (2020) 34 *Body Image* 38, 42.

18 Georgia Wells, Jeff Horwitz and Deepa Seetharaman, 'Facebook Knows Instagram Is Toxic for Teen Girls, Company Documents Show', *Wall Street Journal* (online, 14 September 2021) <https://www.wsj.com/articles/facebook-knows-instagram-is-toxic-for-teen-girls-company-documents-show-11631620739>.

19 Ibid.

20 Jasmine Fardouly and Lenny R Vartanian, 'Negative Comparisons about One's Appearance Mediate the Relationship between Facebook Usage and Body Image Concerns' (2015) 12 *Body Image* 82, 86 ('Negative Comparisons').

21 Fardouly and Vartanian, 'Negative Comparisons' (n 20) 86; Blair C Burnette, Melissa A Kwitowski and Suzanne E Mazzeo, '"I Don't Need People to Tell Me I'm Pretty on Social Media:" A Qualitative Study of Social Media and Body Image in Early Adolescent Girls' (2017) 23 *Body Image* 114, 122.

people'.[22] Research that Ms Haugen leaked stated that using Instagram resulted in body image problems and developing eating disorders, and a study by Instagram staff found that 17% of teenage girls stated that using Instagram worsened their eating disorder.[23]

Social Media, Body Image and the Law

Over 30 relatively recent lawsuits in the United States, with several social media as the defendants, include an allegation that social media contributed to the plaintiff's eating disorder.[24] For example, in *Spence v. Meta Platforms, Inc.*,[25] the plaintiffs, Alexis Spence and her parents, sued Meta for contributing to children and teenagers' poor mental health and for Spence's health problems allegedly caused by using Instagram which included eating disorders, addiction, anxiety and depression, starting when she was 11 years old.[26]

Spence brought several causes of action against Meta. Some of them were: (i) Instagram has a 'defective design' that is 'not reasonably safe for ordinary consumers or minor users'[27] and there are inexpensive ways to make it safer, but Meta's staff decided not to pursue them;[28] (ii) Meta did not provide sufficient warnings to young people and their parents about the possible foreseeable dangers and potential addiction from using Instagram;[29] (iii) negligence; (iii) Instagram is 'unreasonably dangerous' and does not warn parents and minors of the 'dangers' from using it;[30] (iv) unjust enrichment: Meta received

22 Evidence to United States Senate Committee on Commerce, Science and Transportation, United States Congress, Washington D.C., 4 October 2021 (Frances Haugen) 1 <https://www.commerce.senate.gov/services/files/FC8A558E-824E-4914-BEDB-3A7B1190BD49>.

23 Tamsin Rose and Meghna Bali, 'Facebook's Own Research Found Instagram Fuels Eating Disorders in Young People', *Triple J* (6 October 2021) <https://www.abc.net.au/triplej/programs/hack/facebook-whistleblower-says-instagram-content-hurts-teens/13573020>.

24 See e.g., *Heffner v. Meta Platforms, Inc.*, No. 3:22-cv-03849 (N.D. Cal. Aug. 2, 2022), ECF No. 13; *Aranda v. Meta Platforms, Inc.*, No. 3:22-cv-04210 (N.D. Cal. Aug. 2, 2022) No. 3:22-cv-04209 (N.3. Cal. Aug. 2, 2022), ECF No. 13; *Roberts v. Meta Platforms, Inc.*, No. 4:22-cv-04210 (N.D. Cal. Aug. 15, 2022), ECF No. 22; *Wuest v. Meta Platforms, Inc.*, No. 4:22-cv-04283 (N.D. Cal. Aug. 15, 2022) ECF No. 19; *Martin v. Meta Platforms, Inc.*, No. 3:22-cv-04286 (N.D. Cal. Aug 15, 2022), ECF No. 17; *Seekford v. Meta Platfotms, Inc.*, No. 4:22-cv-03883 (N.D. Cal. Aug. 15 2022); *Flatt v. Meta Platforms, Inc. et al.*, No. 3:22-cv-04535 (N.D. Cal Aug. 19, 2022), *MC v. Meta Platforms, Inc. et al.*, No 4:22-cv-04529 (N.D. Cal Aug. 22, 2022), *T.K. v. Meta Platforms, Inc. et al.*, No. 3:22-cv-04588 (N.D. Cal. Sept. 1, 2022). See also *In re Social Media Adolescent Addiction/Personal Injury Products Liability Litigation*, 2024 U.S. Dist. LEXIS 160893.

25 Complaint in *Spence v. Meta Platforms, Inc.*, (N.D. Cal. 2022) (No. 22CV03294), 2022 WL 2101825 [1].

26 Ibid [2]–[3].

27 Ibid [45].

28 Ibid.

29 Ibid [48].

30 Ibid [49].

a 'direct benefit' from Spence spending considerable time on Instagram and creating several accounts;[31] and (v) invasion of privacy: Spence's parents could not 'monitor and control' her social media use.[32]

In a similar lawsuit, *Rodriguez v. Meta Platforms, Inc.*,[33] the plaintiff, Sofia Rodriguez, an adult,[34] sued several social media, including Meta, Tiktok and Bytedance. Rodriguez uses social media very frequently which allegedly caused her social media addiction. She further claimed that she developed many illnesses from using social media, including an eating disorder, body dysmorphia, depression, severe anxiety and self-harm.[35]

Rodriguez sued the social media for various causes of action, including: (i) their creators 'defectively designed the platforms to specifically appeal to and addict minors and young adults, who were particularly unable to appreciate the risks posed by the platforms, and particularly susceptible to harms from those products';[36] and (ii) they did not do enough to warn users about the risk of various issues, including addiction, body dysmorphia, eating disorders, Anorexia Nervosa, suicidal ideation, difficulty sleeping, self-harm and fatigue.[37]

His Honour Magistrate Judge Kang stayed all the lawsuits, including those outlined above.[38] A stay usually involves a judicial officer deciding that a court matter will temporarily not proceed further in the litigation process.[39] In September 2024, His Honour made an order for the plaintiffs and defendants in the cases to confer to discuss issues related to discovery, so as at that date, the lawsuits were still in progress, with no final judgment.[40]

Discovery is a step in the litigation process that occurs in common law systems: the parties to the litigation can be required to give each other, to inspect and copy, all of the documents that they have that contain information that could help the other party further their case or harm the case of the party that gave them the documents.[41]

31 Ibid [51].
32 Ibid [53].
33 *Rodriguez v. Meta Platforms, Inc.*, No. 3:22-cv-00401 (N.D. Cal. Jan. 20, 2022), 2022 WL 190807.
34 Ibid [17].
35 Ibid [100]–[105].
36 Complaint in *Spence v. Meta Platforms, Inc.*, (N.D. Cal. 2022) (No. 22CV03294), 2022 WL 2101825 [113].
37 Ibid [139].
38 *J.H. v. Meta Platforms, Inc.*, 2022 U.S. Dist. LEXIS 169331, [1].
39 *Wex* (online at 12 April 2025) 'stay' < https://www.law.cornell.edu/wex/stay>.
40 *In re Social Media Adolescent Addiction/Personal Injury Products Liability Litigation*, 2024 U.S. Dist. LEXIS 160893.
41 *Expense Reduction Analysts Group Pty Ltd and Others v. Armstrong Strategic Management and Marketing Pty Ltd and Ors* [2013] HCA 46 [44].

In May 2021, over 40 American Attorneys-General wrote a letter to Mark Zuckerberg, CEO of Facebook (now Meta),[42] which stated that social media can harm the physical and mental health of children, and it encourages children to constantly check their social media. It referred to a mistake with Instagram's algorithm which promoted diet content to users who have eating disorders: it recommended terms like appetite suppressant and fasting.[43] Later, in October 2023, over 30 American State Attorneys-General commenced a lawsuit in the American Federal Court in California against Meta. They alleged that Meta created a scheme with four parts; it: (1) developed a business model through Facebook and Instagram to maximise children's time on their social media; (2) created and used features in its products that are harmful to make children become addicted to it, while claiming publicly that it was safe for children; (3) frequently published reports that stated that users of its social media rarely experienced harm; and (4) even though Meta has a substantial amount of evidence that its products cause harm, it refuses to modify its features that it knows cause harm and still represents to the public that it does not harm children.[44]

The complaint filed in the matter alleged that Meta's staff deceive the public by stating in their public communications that Meta does not allow content that promotes eating disorders while they purposely retain features that they know promote eating disorders.[45] Some of the legal remedies they seek include a permanent injunction for Meta to stop its behaviour, damages and restitution.[46]

Conclusion

This chapter discussed how social media can harm body image. It also explained some of the (unresolved at the date of writing) litigation by plaintiffs who allege that social media contributed to their eating disorder. This chapter concludes the parts of this book that comprise the necessary background to try to understand why politicians and advocates have looked to legislative action to try to address the harm that can result from seeing thin-ideal images. The author now invites you to read the next chapter, a comprehensive exploration of Body Image Law.

42 Letter from National Association of Attorneys General to Mark Zuckerberg, 10 May 2021 <https://www.mass.gov/doc/naag-letter-to-facebook/download>.

43 Ibid.

44 *Arizona & Ors v. Meta Platforms, Inc.*, 4:23-cv-05448 (N.D. Cal. Oct. 24, 2023), [2].

45 Ibid [333].

46 Ibid [1171].

5 Body Image Law

A Detailed Examination

Introduction

Australian Senator Helen Polley stated over a decade ago,

> [o]f course, the photoshopping of media images is not the sole contributing factor to the widespread problems of depression, eating disorders and social isolation which plague young people. It has, however, been identified in country after country as a major contributing factor and one which can and should be regulated by responsible governments. It comes as no surprise then that in recent years attempts have been made around the world to introduce legislation mandating that digitally enhanced photographs of models carry disclosure statements. These are statements that would inform consumers that the image they were viewing had been altered and was not an accurate representation of the model photographed.[1]

Senator Polley described part of what is now known as Body Image Law. The parts of the Body Image Law definition that this book will examine in detail (as stated in Chapter 1) are: (1) models needing to have a minimum body mass index ('BMI') to work; and (2) requiring editors and other pertinent people to post a disclaimer on images of people who they digitally altered to appear thinner.[2] The main aim of Body Image Law is to create legislation and/or policy that reduces, or even eliminates, the use of thin-ideal images and the idealisation of the Thin-Ideal, and/or that results in these images having a lesser negative impact on body image and being less likely to contribute to developing eating disorders.

1 Commonwealth, *Parliamentary Debates*, Senate, 21 November 2022, 9355 (Helen Polley) <https://parlinfo.aph.gov.au/parlInfo/download/chamber/hansards/dcbf3820-67a9-494a-bf57-5efe0c27f413/toc_pdf/Senate_2012_11_21_1526_Official.pdf;fileType=application%2Fpdf>.

2 Marilyn Bromberg and Cindy Halliwell, "All About That Bass' and Photoshopping a Model's Waist: Introducing Body Image Law' (2016) 18 *Notre Dame Law Review* 1, 2.

DOI: 10.4324/9781003678793-5

These laws are alternatively referred to as 'photoshop laws';[3] however, the author prefers to use the term 'Body Image Law'. 'Photoshop laws' is a narrow term: it only refers to the component of the laws concerned with adding a disclaimer to images that were digitally modified. In contrast, the term 'Body Image Law' is broader, so other relevant initiatives that could help to improve body image would fall under it.

As a result of Body Image Law's 'novelty, however, its sphere of application and its efficacy remain largely unclear and the law is therefore likely to be misunderstood by laypersons'.[4] One of the aims of this chapter is to clarify its sphere of application and the next chapter will explain its efficacy.

This chapter will discuss the Body Image Laws that were passed, then it will examine the Body Image Laws that were proposed that were not passed (bills), then it will consider government and industry policies and actions that appear similar to Body Image Law (e.g. the owners of a business deciding that they will not digitally alter the bodies of models in their photos, without any legislation requiring them to). After this, it will explain self-regulation in advertising industries that are similar in spirit to Body Image Law.

Body Image Laws That Were Passed

The First Federal Body Image Law That Was Passed (of Three): The Israeli Body Image Law

In 2013, the Israeli Government was the first federal government in the world known to the author to pass a Body Image Law in the form of federal legislation. The law requires models to have a minimum BMI of 18.5 to work: they must obtain a certificate from their doctor confirming this before they can work.[5] It also requires that if an image was modified to make the model in it look thinner, it must have a disclaimer stating that it was altered.[6] Adi Barkan, an Israeli fashion photographer, initially had the idea for this law, after a model friend of his died from Anorexia Nervosa in 2007, and Dr Rachel Adato, a medical doctor who was a member

3 See, for example, Talya Minsberg, 'What the US Can – and Can't – Learn from Israel's Ban on Ultra-Thin Models', *The Atlantic* (online, 9 May 2012) <https://www.theatlantic.com/international/archive/2012/05/what-the-us-can-and-cant-learn-from-israels-ban-on-ultra-thin-models/256891/>.

4 Philippa Anna Attrill, 'Towards the Development of Photoshop Law and Its Enforceability within the European Union' (Masters Thesis, Tallinn University of Technology, 2023) 12.

5 לקשמ תלבגה קוח תעצה תונמגודה ףנעב [Law for Restricting Weight in the Modelling Industry], 27 March 2012, 5772-2012 ss 1, 2(a).

6 Ibid s 3.

of the Israeli Parliament ('Knesset') at the time, introduced the law in Parliament.[7]

The bill originally included fines as a penalty for breaching it, but this was removed before the final version of the bill went to the Knesset.[8] The final version of the law does not have penalties for breach.[9] Instead, those claiming to be wronged as a result of an advertisement that breached the law can commence a class action.[10] The initial version of the law forbade any editing of models' bodies in images and Israeli politicians later replaced this by requiring a disclaimer on images containing models' bodies that were digitally altered (which was included in the version of the law that was passed).[11]

Supporters of the bill, including the Israeli Association for Eating Disorders, argued that not supporting it

> would result in direct and irreversible harm to an entire population of young, pre-adolescent, and adolescent girls who are internalizing unrealistic messages that may hurt their self-confidence, self-worth, and body image, beginning at a very young age. Youngsters might not know what is real and what is unreal and may end up experiencing body dissatisfaction, feeling unworthy, and starting habits at a young age for losing and regulating weight that can be irreversibly harmful.[12]

Importantly, the Israeli Body Image Law resulted in increased public awareness about disordered eating and eating disorders.[13] During the Healthy Weight Week in the United States, an award was given to the Israeli Government for passing its Body Image Law.[14] *Vogue* magazine staff supported the Israeli Body Image Law and announced that they would not use

7 Yael Latzer, Rachel Adatto and Dianne Neumark-Sztainer, 'Addressing Eating Disorders through Legislation: The Israeli "Models' Law" Process, Enactment, and Dilemmas' (2022) 1 *Dialogues in Health* 1, 2 ('Addressing Eating Disorders'); Center for Israel Education, 'Knesset Passes "Photoshop Law" (Web Page, 19 March 2012) <https://israeled.org/knesset-passes-photoshop-law/>.

8 Renana Gutreich, *Implementation and Enforcement of the Law for Restricting Weight in the Modeling Industry, 5772-2012* (The Knesset Research and Information Center, 7 June 2017) 5 <https://m.knesset.gov.il/EN/activity/mmm/me04076.pdf>.

9 Ibid.

10 Ibid.

11 Latzer, Adatto and Neumark-Sztainer (n 7) 2; Gutreich (n 8) 12.

12 Latzer, Adatto and Neumark-Sztainer (n 7) 3.

13 Center for Israel Education (n 6); Michal Cohen and Yael Latzer, 'The Impact of Israel's "Models' Law" on Young Women' (2021) *International Journal of Psychological Studies* 32, 34 ("The Impact"); Latzer, Adatto and Neumark-Sztainer, 'Addressing Eating Disorders through Legislation' (n 7) 4.

14 Latzer, Adatto and Neumark-Sztainer, 'Addressing Eating Disorders through Legislation' (n 7) 4.

images of underweight models who appeared to have eating disorders and models under age 16.[15]

Researchers studied the impact of the Israeli Body Image Law, about eight years after it came into effect.[16] They found that most survey participants, regardless of age, had heard of the law and supported it.[17] The study had two age groups: younger participants, aged 18–24, and older participants, aged 25–35.[18] About 26% of the younger participants stated that they moderately changed their beliefs about the thin-ideal and its impact on health due to the law, compared to 21.31% of the older participants.[19] Most of the study participants supported enforcing the law and creating further legislation in the area.[20] This survey is significant, because it is a rare example of evidence that shows that the existence of Body Image Law can itself result in psychological improvements on body image-related issues.

The survey also assessed feelings towards the Body Image Law overall. It did not assess sentiment towards one of the two main limbs of the Israeli Body Image Law specifically (either the minimum BMI obligation for models or the requirement for a disclaimer on images of models that advertisers digitally altered).[21] It would be helpful to know the specific impact each of the law's two limbs had on the survey participants to extrapolate whether one is more beneficial to improve body image and provide data for politicians in other jurisdictions to support their deciding whether they should consider replicating one limb of the law, as opposed to both. The author hypothesises that it would not be the part of the law that requires a disclaimer on models whose image was digitally altered, because there is compelling research that they are ineffective, which this book will discuss in Chapter 6. Also, the survey did not assess the impact that the Israeli law had on the eating disorder behaviour of the survey participants. This would be helpful to learn to assess whether Body Image Law is accomplishing its goals: one of such goals is to create legislation and/or policy that results in there being less thin-ideal images and/or that these images are less likely to contribute to poor body image or developing eating disorders.

15 Ibid 4.
16 See Cohen and Latzer, 'The Impact' (n 13) 32.
17 Ibid 43.
18 Ibid 43.
19 Ibid 43–44.
20 Ibid.
21 ןנ תונמגודה תעצה קוח תלבגה לקשמ [Law for Restricting Weight in the Modelling Industry], 27 March 2012, 5772-2012 ss 1, 2(a), 3.

In 2022, an amendment to the Israeli Body Image Law was proposed in the Knesset,[22] but it did not pass.[23] The amendment stated that the Israeli Government would be responsible for enforcing the law and breaching it would result in receiving a fine (and the money would go towards preventing and treating eating disorders and reimbursing people who were harmed from breaching the law). Moreover, the offender's details would be listed on the website of the Ministry of Economy of Industry.[24]

A person who had severe Anorexia for more than 15 years, but recovered, started a class action lawsuit, pursuant to the Israeli Body Image Law, in about 2018. A well-known lawyer represented her and argued that media messages contributed to her developing and sustaining an eating disorder.[25] The lawsuit was against a news company and a lingerie company for breaching the Israeli Body Image Law, but the plaintiff withdrew her application. The Court dismissed the case and ordered the plaintiff to pay 7,000 (NIS) in costs to the defendants.[26] It is possible that this case, in which a judicial officer ordered the plaintiff in a Body Image Law lawsuit to pay costs to defendants, may discourage others from commencing such a lawsuit. Starting a lawsuit can be challenging on one's resources, including their time, and it can be emotionally draining, but the possibility of paying costs to the opposing party is a further matter that can deter other potential plaintiffs from starting similar litigation. The author searched legal databases in June 2025 to find the reason why the plaintiff withdrew the lawsuit and more information about the case, but she could not find anything.

The author could only find one lawsuit that commenced pursuant to the Israeli Body Image Law. This appears to indicate that it may be more symbolic than legally effective. Indeed, the explanatory notes to the proposed 2016 amendment to the law state that 'despite Israel being a pioneer in this area of legislation, it still lags behind the developing standard in the world, as it has not yet enacted measures to enforce and supervise the law'.[27]

22 שונות הוראות – תיקון הדוגמנות בענף משקל הגבלת חוק צעת [Law for Restricting Weight in the Modelling Industry] [(Amendment – Various Provisions)], 2 September 2022, 5776-2016 (P/2825/20).

23 'חוק הצעות' [Laws], *knesset.gov.il* <https://main.knesset.gov.il:443/Activity/Legislation/Laws/pages/lawsuggestionssearch.aspx?t=lawsuggestionssearch&st=allsuggestions&wn=%D7%93%D7%95%D7%92%D7%9E%D7%A0%D7%95%D7%AA&ki=-1&sb=latestsessiondate&so=d>.

24 שונות הוראות – תיקון הדוגמנות בענף משקל הגבלת חוק הצעת [Law for Restricting Weight in the Modelling Industry] [(Amendment – Various Provisions)], 2 September 2022, 5776-2016 (P/2825/20) s 6A.

25 Latzer, Adatto and Neumark-Sztainer, 'Addressing Eating Disorders through Legislation' (n 7) 5.

26 מרכז-לוד המחוזי המשפט בית [Central District Court of Lod], Case No. 61161-03-19, 3 June 2021 (Is).

27 שונות הוראות – תיקון הדוגמנות בענף משקל הגבלת חוק הצעת [Law for Restricting Weight in the Modelling Industry] [(Amendment – Various Provisions)], 2 September 2022, 5776-2016 (P/2825/20).

When legal changes occur, this does not, of course, necessarily mean that cultural changes on the same issue occur.[28] Lawyer and activist Thomas B. Stoddard stated that law can change culture[29] when it 'express[es] a new moral ideal or standard' and changes 'cultural attitudes and functions'.[30] He gave anti-smoking laws as an example of 'culture-shifting' law because they affected people's everyday lives and resulted in less people smoking.[31] For a law to be 'culture-shifting', it must be 'known, accepted and enforced'.[32] Enforcing a law must be 'multifaced, realistic and continuous' and increases the chances that a law will be 'culture-shifting'.[33] If a government does not enforce a law, then people may be more likely to ignore part or all of it.[34] Laws that the legislature made, rather than case law by the courts, are most likely to result in 'culture-shifting' law.[35]

In terms of Body Image Law, passing such a law does not mean (like any law) that all people will abide by it, particularly if culture does not change to worship the thin-ideal less. It is possible, though, that a Body Image Law, if actively enforced, might of itself help to modify culture, because, applying Stoddard's reasoning, it could create a new moral standard, changing people's views of the thin-ideal as the beauty standard and cultural attitudes towards women's bodies.

The Second Federal Body Image Law That Was Passed (of Three): The French Body Image Law

France is critical to the fashion industry.[36] French Senator Valerie Boyer introduced a Body Image Law in the French Parliament in 2009. The bill required a warning to be added on images of models that were modified, and it applied to advertisements, press photos, political campaigns, art photography and product packaging.[37] Fines for breaching the bill were 37,500 Euro,

28 Thomas B Stoddard, 'Bleeding Heart: Reflections on Using the Law to Make Social Change' (1997) 72(5) *New York University Law Review* 966, 970.
29 Ibid 977–978.
30 Ibid 972.
31 Ibid 979.
32 Ibid 980.
33 Ibid 987.
34 Ibid 986.
35 Ibid 991.
36 Katherine L Record and Bryn S Austin, '"Paris Thin": A Call to Regulate Life-Threatening Starvation of Runway Models in the US Fashion Industry' (2016) 106(2) *American Journal of Public* 205, 205.
37 Commonwealth, *Parliamentary Debates*, Senate, 21 November 2022, 9355 (Helen Polley); *Proposition de loi relative aux photographies d'images Corporelles Retouchées* [Proposed Law on Retouched Body Image Photographs] (France), 15 September 2009, N° 1908 <https://www.assemblee-nationale.fr/13/propositions/pion1908.asp>.

which could increase to 50% of the amount spent on advertising.[38] More than 50 other French legislators supported the bill and it passed the French Lower House of Parliament, but not the Upper House, so it did not become law.[39]

Later, in 2017, the French Government successfully passed a different Body Image Law from the one introduced in 2009, which is fairly similar to the Israeli Body Image Law. It has two limbs: models must provide a medical certificate to work which says that the model's health, which is assessed with specifically considering their BMI, is compatible with their profession (and it stated that a decree from the Ministers for Health and Labour would explain this further);[40] and images in which a model's body shape was changed must have a disclaimer which states 'photographie retouchée' (retouched photograph).[41] The French law does not state any requirements regarding the format of the label or how it should be positioned, in contrast to the Israeli law.[42] The French law (unlike the Israeli law) is criminal: penalties for breaching it include fines and imprisonment. If a person posts an image of a model that was modified without the required disclaimer, they can be fined 37,500 Euro or 30% of the amount that they spent on advertising.[43] If a French modelling agency receives money from one of their models who does not have the required medical certificate, its staff can face a sentence of six months in prison and a 75,000 Euro fine.[44] Another component of the French Body Image Law, which this book will discuss in Chapter 7, deals with criminal sanctions for people who post Pro-Anorexia content online.[45]

Dr Olivier Veran, a doctor and French politician, introduced the French Body Image Law.[46] He stated that '[w]e want to combat the idea that an agency could urge a model to stop eating; for example eating cotton balls to lose their appetite, to always lose more weight'.[47] The National Union of

38 *Proposition de loi relative aux photographies d'images corporelles retouchées* [Proposed Law on Retouched Body Image Photographs] (France), 15 September 2009, N° 1908 <https://www.assemblee-nationale.fr/13/propositions/pion1908.asp>.

39 Ashley O'Neil, 'A Call for Truth in the Fashion Pages: What Global Trend in Advertising Regulation Means for U.S. Beauty and Fashion Advertisers' (2014) 21(2) *Indiana Journal of Global Legal Studies* 619, 628, 629.

40 *Code du travail* [Labour Code] (France) art L. 7123-2-1.

41 *Code de la santé publique* [Public Health Code] (France) art L. 2133-2.

42 Rachel F Rodgers and Katherine Laveway, 'Retouchée au Féminin: The Gendered Nature of the French Law Mandating Labeling of Digitally Modified Images' (2021) 10(62) *Laws* 1, 3.

43 *Code de La Santé Publique* [Public Health Code] (France) art 2133-2.

44 *Code Du Travail* [Labour Code] (France) art L. 7123-27; Connor Bildfell, 'Legislating Away Illness: Examining Efforts to Curb the Development of Eating Disorders through Law' (2018) 26 *Dalhousie Journal of Legal Studies* 37, 51.

45 *Loi n° 2016-41 du 26 Janvier 2016 de modernisation de notre système de santé* [Law No 2016-41 of 26 January 2016 on the Modernisation of Our Health System] (France).

46 Erin McLaughlin and Sandrine Amiel, 'France Weighs Skinny Model Ban' (online, 17 March 2015) <https://edition.cnn.com/2015/03/17/europe/france-skinny-model-ban/index.html>

47 Ibid.

Modelling Agencies in France argued that the French Body Image Law would make French modelling less competitive.[48]

Researchers asked models who participated in Fashion Week in New York in 2018 about whether they planned to participate in Fashion Week in Paris and if so, whether they obtained a health certificate for it and which health indicators their doctor assessed.[49] Fifteen of the models stated that they planned to participate in French Fashion Week in Paris and all 15 stated that they obtained a health certificate for it. Most stated that their doctor examined their weight, blood pressure, pulse and heart rate. Only a few stated that their doctor asked about issues related to eating disorders.[50] This suggests that the law may be successful in getting models to see a medical professional to obtain the certificate, but doctors likely need some training concerning how they assess models.[51] Nevertheless, it appears positive that doctors assessed the indicators mentioned, which are relevant to their overall health, as those factors may also be pertinent to whether or not their body looks like the thin-ideal. For example, if a doctor is satisfied with a model's weight (one of the indicators mentioned), it could be that it is less likely that they look like the thin-ideal.

In 2023, the French Government passed a law concerning influencers;[52] this was its second law concerning influencers: it first passed a law focusing on child influencers in 2020.[53] The 2023 French law had a few brief parts related to body image: it stated that if influencers digitally alter an image to make a silhouette look thinner or thicker or digitally alter a face, it requires a statement that says 'retouched image'.[54] Also, if an influencer uses artificial intelligence to create a face or silhouette, it needs to have the phrase 'virtual image'.[55] The statements that the influencers add to the images must be clear

48 'French MPs Back Ban on Skinny Catwalk Models', *BBC News* (online, 3 April 2015) <https://www.bbc.com/news/world-europe-32174364>.

49 Rachel F Rodgers et al, 'Disordered Eating Behaviors and Sexual Objectification during New York Fashion Week: Implementation of Industry Policies and Legislation' (2021) 54(3) *The International Journal of Eating Disorders* 433, 435.

50 Ibid.

51 Ibid 436.

52 *Loi no 2023-451 du juin 2023 visant à encadrer l'influence commerciale et à lutter contre les dérives des influenceurs sur les réseaux sociaux* (France) JO, 10 juin 2023, no 0133, texte no 1.

53 *Loi no 2020-1266 du octobre 2020 visant à encadrer l'exploitation commerciale de l'image d'enfants de moins de seize ans sur les plateformes en ligne* (France) JO, 20 octobre 2020, no 0255, text no 1.

54 *Loi no 2023-451 du juin 2023 visant à encadrer l'influence commerciale et à lutter contre les dérives des influenceurs sur les réseaux sociaux* (France) JO, 10 juin 2023, no 0133, texte no 1, s 2, art 5 II(1).

55 Ibid s 2, art 5 II(2).

and legible.[56] Influencers who breach this law can face one year in prison and a 4,500 Euro fine.[57]

While the 2023 French law regarding influencers is mostly a law about influencers, it can still be considered a Body Image Law. If you revert back to the definition of a Body Image Law from earlier in this chapter, it states that it includes

> the bills, laws and government actions (such as establishing parliamentary inquiries and creating policies) that may help to improve the body image of the general public, and particularly of young people…Body Image Law can include measures such as:…(2) requiring editors and other relevant people to post a warning on images of people who they have photoshopped to appear thinner.[58]

Since the 2023 French law concerning influencers involves adding a statement to an image when an influencer modified it and one of the possible modifications that could have occurred was the model was digitally altered to appear thinner, you could infer that the French Government would have created this part of the law to improve the body image of the public. Consequently, it appears to be a Body Image Law. Further, this legislative requirement appears very similar to the part of the original French Body Image Law that requires a disclaimer.

It is interesting that the 2023 French Influencer Law is the first law in the world, to the author's knowledge, that states that if artificial intelligence was used to create a face or silhouette, it requires a particular statement. The final chapter of this book will discuss using artificial intelligence to create models and the connection to Body Image Law.

The Third Federal Body Image Law That Was Passed (of Three): The Norwegian Body Image Law

In 2011, the Norwegian Minister for Children and Equality, Audun Lysbakken, advocated for disclaimers to help people learn which images were altered and which were not.[59] Later, in 2021, the Norwegian Government passed a Body

56 Ibid s 2, art 5 .

57 Ibid s 2, art 5 IV.

58 Bromberg and Halliwell (n 2) 2.

59 'Commonwealth, *Parliamentary Debates*, Senate, 21 November 2022, 9355 (Helen Polley)' <https://parlinfo.aph.gov.au/parlInfo/download/chamber/hansards/dcbf3820-67a9-494a-bf57-5efe0c27f413/toc_pdf/Senate_2012_11_21_1526_Official.pdf;fileType=application%2Fpdf>; 'Put Warning Labels on Skinny Models: Minister', *The Local Norway* (online, 10 November 2011) <https://www.thelocal.no/20111110/put-warning-labels-on-skinny-models>.

Image Law by amending its Marketing Control Act (2009). The law states that when advertisers digitally alter a person's body shape, size or skin, they must add a disclaimer stating this. It further said that it would also pass regulations regarding implementing the law, including its exemptions.[60] If someone breaches this law intentionally or negligently and it occurs significantly or repeatedly, they may be fined.[61] The law does not state the fine amount. Nor does the law define 'intentionally', 'negligently', 'significantly' or 'repeatedly', which can help people abide by it. The disclaimer affects anyone who posts on social media and is paid for it, which includes actors, musicians and influencers,[62] if they received a benefit or payment relating to the post.[63]

Norwegian Government Guidelines explain that the purpose of the Norwegian Body Image Law

> is to combat body-image pressure in society which can be attributed to idealized people in advertising. The requirement to label retouched or manipulated advertising is set to raise awareness among consumers, particularly children and youths, that the persons in the advertisement deviate from reality. The aim is to reduce the use of idealized bodies that are retouched in advertising.[64]

The law also stated that the Norwegian Ministry of Children and Family Affairs will create a standardised disclaimer for advertisers to use, the Norwegian Consumer Agency will enforce the law and people can appeal the decisions to the Norwegian Market Council.[65] Government regulations and guidelines pursuant to the law include the standardised disclaimer, which is round and says, in Norwegian, 'retouched person advertising'.[66] They add

60 *Lov Om Endringer i Markedsføringsloven mv. (Merking Av Retusjert Reklame)* [Act on Amendments to the Marketing Act, etc. (Labelling of Retouched Advertising)] (Norway), 11 June 2021, No. 62, § 2.

61 Ibid § 42.

62 Kirsty Grant, 'Influencers React to Norway Photo Edit Law: "Welcome Honesty" or a "Shortcut"?', *BBC* (online, 7 July 2021) <https://www.bbc.com/news/newsbeat-57721080>.

63 Gabriel Geiger, 'Norway Law Forces Influencers to Label Retouched Photos on Instagram', *VICE* (online, 29 June 2021) <https://www.vice.com/en/article/norway-law-forces-influencers-to-label-retouched-photos-on-instagram/>.

64 'The Norwegian Consumer Authority's Guideline on Labelling Retouched Advertising', *Forbrukertilsynet* (25 January 2023) <https://www.forbrukertilsynet.no/english/guidelines/the-norwegian-consumer-authoritys-guideline-on-labelling-retouched-advertising>.

65 Barne-og familiedepartementet [Ministry of Children and Family Affairs], 'Retusjert reklame må merkjast [Retouched advertising must be marked]', *Regjeringa.no* (9 April 2021) <https://www.regjeringen.no/nn/dokumentarkiv/regjeringa-solberg/aktuelt-regjeringen-solberg/aktuelt5/nyheiter/2021/retusjert-reklame-ma-merkjast/id2843545/>.

66 'The Norwegian Consumer Authority's Guideline on Labelling Retouched Advertising' (n 64).

that the disclaimer needs to cover about 7% of the image that it is on.[67] The guidelines also state that the disclaimer must be in the upper left corner of the advertising and needs to contrast with the background.[68]

Norwegian Minister of Consumer Affairs Kjell Ingolf Ropstad said the following about the law:

> [w]e take body pressure seriously. The proposal for a duty to label retouched advertising is part of the government's work against physical and appearance pressure. The proposal also means that the requirements for marketing aimed at children will be stricter, because it will be assessed whether the marketing contributes to body pressure…I want children and young people to grow up without experiencing pressure to change their body to be 'good enough'.[69]

The Norwegian Body Image Law is the first Body Image Law in the world passed (to the author's knowledge) that addresses digitally altering skin. It is understandable why the Norwegian Government included skin in its Body Image Law. When people digitally alter images, they can change, among other things, the model's body and their skin,[70] and there is pressure on women to have flawless skin.[71] Healthy skin can affect well-being, sexual attractiveness and self-esteem.[72] The portrayal of skin in mass media has resulted in some women thinking that their skin must look perfect.[73] The impact of the skin component of the Norwegian Body Image Law and an analysis of whether Body Image Laws generally should address digitally modifying models' skin is outside the purview of this book because it is beyond the author's expertise. It is, nevertheless, an important issue to consider for many reasons, such as the pressure on women to have perfect skin and the ubiquitous digital altering of models' skin in advertisements.

67 'The Norwegian Consumer Authority's Guideline on Labelling Retouched Advertising' (n 64); *Forskrift Om Merking Av Retusjert Reklame [Regulations on the Labelling of Retouched Advertising] 2022* (Norway), 17 June 2022, FOR-2022-06-17-1114 § 1.

68 'The Norwegian Consumer Authority's Guideline on Labelling Retouched Advertising' (n 64).

69 Barne-og familiedepartementet [Ministry of Children and Family Affairs] (n 65).

70 Fiona MacCallum et al, 'Altered Images: Understanding the Influence of Unrealistic Images and Beauty Aspirations' (2018) 26(3) *Health Care Analysis* 235, 235–236.

71 See, for example, Sue Jackson and Tiina Vares, '"Perfect Skin", "Pretty Skinny": Girls' Embodied Identities and Post-Feminist Popular Culture' (2015) 24(3) *Journal of Gender Studies* 347, 357–358.

72 Anargyros Kouris et al, 'Patients' Self-Esteem before and After Chemical Peeling Procedure' (2018) 20(4) *Journal of Cosmetic and Laser Therapy* 220, 221.

73 Parker Magin et al, '"Perfect Skin", the Media and Patients with Skin Disease: A Qualitative Study of Patients with Acne, Psoriasis and Atopic Eczema' (2011) 17(2) *Australian Journal of Primary Health* 181, 183.

It would be easier to hold people who breach the French or Norwegian Body Image Laws to account than the Israeli Body Image Law, since the French or Norwegian Governments would have the resources to charge alleged offenders whereas the average Israeli would have to commence a class action lawsuit at their own risk and cost. Israeli legislators appeared to be aware that their legislation had no teeth in the explanatory notes to their proposed amendments to their original Body Image Law.[74]

This hypothesis, however, would depend on the priority that the French and Norwegian Governments give to these laws in allocating resources: if they do not provide resources to the appropriate people to investigate breaches of these laws and charge them, then in reality, people will not be punished for breaching them, and once people recognise this, it could affect the deterrent effect of a Body Image Law.

Body Image Laws That Were Proposed but Not Passed

This section of the book will describe bills that were proposed as Body Image Laws but did not become law. The purpose of this section is to show different versions of Body Image Law than those previously described, to try to ensure this book's value as a resource by comprehensively including all attempts to pass Body Image Law worldwide and to make this book's later discussion of whether Body Image Law should exist at all more robust.

Types of Body Image Bills That Did Not Pass (Number One): Bills That Proposed Warnings on Images

In 2009, U.K. Member of Parliament (M.P.) Jo Swinson tried to introduce legislation in Parliament that required advertisers to add a disclaimer to images in advertisements that were photoshopped that stated that they were photoshopped.[75] The bill would have also banned all modified images in advertisements that targeted children under 16. Each advertisement with modified images would have required a warning that would rate it between 1 and 4, depending on the amount of retouching. A 4 would signify the greatest amount of retouching, whereas a 1 would be used for small changes, like to lighting or the background.[76] More recently in the United Kingdom, in 2020, Dr Luke

74 תונוש תוארוה – ןוקית תונמגודה ףנעב לקשמ תלבגה קוח תעצה [Law for Restricting Weight in the Modelling Industry] [(Amendment – Various Provisions)], 2 September 2022, 5776-2016 (P/2825/20), explanatory notes.

75 Commonwealth, *Parliamentary Debates*, Senate, 21 November 2022, 9355 (Helen Polley) <https://parlinfo.aph.gov.au/parlInfo/download/chamber/hansards/dcbf3820-67a9-494a-bf57-5efe0c27f413/toc_pdf/Senate_2012_11_21_1526_Official.pdf;fileType=application%2Fpdf>.

76 O'Neil (n 39) 626.

Evans M.P. proposed a bill which required advertisers, broadcasters and publishers to add a logo onto an image when technology modified a human body or body part stating that it was altered. The bill made it to the second reading in the House of Commons, but no further.[77] The Girl Guides organisation in the United Kingdom supported the bill.[78]

In 2010, in Brazil, Wladimir Costa, who was a member of the Brazilian Chamber of Deputies at the time, proposed a bill that would require a disclaimer on images of models in which the model's physical image was digitally altered.[79] The warning would state 'attention: image retouched to alter the physical appearance of the person portrayed' and would apply to campaign photos, photography, product packaging and advertising.[80] The text would have been required to be visible and proportional to the rest of the image.[81] Breaching the law could have resulted in a fine of up to 50% of the advertising cost.[82] The bill did not become law.[83]

In Arizona, in 2012, Representative Katie Hobbs proposed a Body Image Law that would require a disclaimer on altered images, which stated '[p]ostproduction techniques were made to alter the appearance in this advertisement. When using this product, similar results may not be achieved'.[84] The Arizona Attorney General would have been responsible for enforcing the law, if it passed, but it did not.[85]

In Ontario, Canada, in 2018, Member of Provincial Parliament Yvan Baker proposed a bill that would compel people who publish photographs or videos for commercial use that they digitally alter to include a disclaimer on the text that states that it was modified.[86] It also required the Ontario Minister of Government and Consumer Services to run an annual eating disorder awareness campaign.[87] Further, it gave power to the Ontario Minister of Health and

77 UK Parliament, 'Digitally Altered Body Images Bill' (Web Page, 4 May 2021) <https://bills.parliament.uk/bills/2778>.

78 Cristina Criddle, *'Girl Guides: Enhanced Photos Need Labels on Social Media', BBC* (online, 3 September 2020) <https://www.bbc.com/news/technology-54003536>.

79 'PL 6.853/2010', *Câmara dos Deputados* [Chamber of Deputies] (5 March 2010) <https://www.camara.leg.br/proposicoesWeb/prop_mostrarintegra?codteor=1246343&filename=Avulso%20PL%206853/2010>; *Projeto De Lei N.° 6.853-B, De 2010* [Bill No. 6,853-B, 2010] (Brazil), 24 February 2010, art 1.

80 *Projeto De Lei N.° 6.853-B, De 2010* [Bill No. 6,853-B, 2010] (Brazil), 24 February 2010, art 2.

81 Ibid art 2 § 1.

82 Ibid art 3.

83 Portal da Câmara dos Deputados [Chamber of Deputies], 'PL 6853/2010 Projecto de Lei', (Web Page) <https://www.camara.leg.br/proposicoesWeb/fichadetramitacao?idProposicao=467269>.

84 House Bill 2793, An Act Requiring Disclaimers on Digitally Altered Advertising Images, 50th Leg, 2nd Reg Sess (Ariz, 2012).

85 Ibid.

86 *Combatting Eating Disorders in Ontario Act, 2018,* Bill 29, 41st Leg, 3rd Sess, Ontario, 2018, s 2(2).

87 Ibid s 5.

Long-Term Care to provide awards to individuals who tried to help lower the number of people with eating disorders.[88] The bill did not become law.[89] Part of this bill is unique in giving awards to people who try to help lower the number of individuals with eating disorders. This bill partially proposed a carrot approach to tackle the problem of the impact of seeing thin-ideal images, whereas normally Body Image Law uses a stick. This then raises the question of whether a carrot or stick approach is better for Body Image Law. The author believes that it is more helpful to consider the potential effectiveness of a specific legislative action or combination thereof to achieve Body Image Law's goals, rather than whether it takes an encouraging or punitive approach. Chapter 8 considers these possible approaches, including their legal feasibility.

Types of Body Image Bills That Did Not Pass (Number Two): Bills That Involved Models Obtaining Health Certificates

In California, Assemblymember Marc Levine proposed a bill with major changes to the modelling industry. Part of the bill stated that the staff of modelling agencies could only hire models who have health certificates from a doctor that stated that the model was 'in healthy physical condition'.[90] Regulations would have been drafted that stated the requirements for the health certificates.[91] If modelling agencies hired models without the health certificates, they would be guilty of a crime and could receive a maximum fine of $5,000.[92] A model would have been required to make their medical records available to the doctor and the doctor would have reviewed them before providing the health certificate.[93] Models would have also been required to have a minimum of three medical checkups per year and meet with a nutritionist.[94] It also required models to be classified as employees, not independent contractors, to give them more rights.[95]

Assemblymember Levine said,

88 Ibid s 6.

89 Legislative Assembly of Ontario, 'Bill 29, Combatting Eating Disorders in Ontario Act, 2018' (Web Page) <https://www.ola.org/en/legislative-business/bills/parliament-41/session-3/bill-29/status>.

90 Assembly Bill 2539, An Act to Add Section 1812.610 to the Civil Code, Relating to Employment of Models, 2015-16 Reg Sess, California, 2016 § 1707.4.

91 Ibid § 1707.5.

92 Ibid § 1707.2.

93 Ibid § 1707.4.

94 Ibid § 1707.5.

95 Ibid § 1707.2.

> [t]he evidence of eating disorders in the modeling industry is alarming. AB 2539 will make sure that models are not enduring physical harm as a workplace prerequisite. This is a societal problem as unhealthy models have become role models for young people. As California often leads the nation and the world, this bill will help assure that our children will see healthy images on magazines and fashion websites.[96]

This bill appears similar to the limb of the Israeli and French Body Image Laws that require a certificate from a doctor to work. Assemblymember Levine worked with eating disorder advocacy group STRIPED, the National Eating Disorders Association and Model Alliance on this bill.[97] STRIPED is the Strategic Training Initiative for the Prevention of Eating Disorders, a cross-disciplinary public health incubator devoted to eating disorders prevention based at the Harvard T.H. Chan School of Public Health and Boston Children's Hospital.[98]

The California Government did not pass the bill, likely due to lobbying from the fashion industry.[99] Any government that seeks to pass a Body Image Law would probably face opposition from the fashion and advertising industries, so it is important to try to obtain the industry's input (and possibly even their support) when creating a Body Image Law. It is also important for those who support a proposed Body Image Law to have strong counterarguments ready to the likely arguments from the fashion and advertising industries. Nevertheless, industry opposition should not prevent politicians from creating a Body Image Law: it is hoped that lawmakers would put the health of the public above potential losses of industry profits and lack of industry favour. Politicians did so in other public health areas, such as smoking, which resulted in significant improvements in health at a macro level.

Two years later, the California Government passed a law, also proposed by Assemblymember Levine, that required the staff of talent agencies to make educational information about nutrition and eating disorders available to models within 90 days of a talent agency agreeing to represent them. The training information would have had to include at least specific information from the National Institute of Health's Eating Disorders website and been

96 'California Assemblymember Proposes Legislation to Create Health Standards for Models', *ABC30 Fresno* (online, 23 February 2016) <https://abc30.com/marc-levine-assemblymember-california-ab-2539/1213519/>.

97 STRIPED, 'Protecting Fashion Model Health' (Web Page) <https://hsph.harvard.edu/research/eating-disorders-striped/policy-translation/protecting-fashion-model-health/>.

98 STRIPED, 'About Us' (Web Page) <https://hsph.harvard.edu/research/eating-disorders-striped/about/>.

99 Erin E. Meyers, 'Fashioning Worker Protections to Combat the Thin Ideal's Cost on Fashion Models and Public Health' (2020) 20 *Vanderbilt Journal of Entertainment and Technology Law* 1219, 1251.

in a language that models understood.[100] It also made it necessary for training materials related to preventing and dealing with sexual harassment to be provided to models.[101] The law did not include the requirements for models to get regular checkups and to provide a health certificate to work that the earlier version did. The law, as it passed, appears to be more palatable to the fashion industry, because it does not require models to take any action; they can ignore the training material if they so chose (though you would hope that they would not) and they would not need to see any doctors or contemplate the state of their health.

The California Bill was unique in that it focused on models' safety and their working conditions: it tried to protect models, as opposed to protecting the public who view thin-ideal images.[102] This raises the question of whether the aim of Body Image Law should be broadened to include trying to improve models' health, and if so, how much of a priority politicians should give it.

Fashion models face considerable pressure from their agents and others to lose weight and maintain it.[103] Their self-esteem can be tied to their weight, which can impact their eating.[104] Researchers found that in face-to-face interviews, models were more likely than non-models to state that they experienced eating disorder symptoms.[105] Another research study found that the 179 models in the study had much higher rates of Anorexia Nervosa than the 261 participants in the control group.[106] Further, researchers found that models during New York Fashion Week in 2018 had 'unhealthy weight control behavio[u]r' at 'concerning' rates and experienced significant pressure to be thin, which demonstrated that models work in unsafe conditions.[107] About 39% of the models in this study used intravenous drips to lower their appetite and give them nutrition so they did not need to eat food.[108] With this in mind, ideally, Body Image Law should address both the negative impact of seeing thin-ideal images while also trying to improve models' health as a priority.

100 Assembly Bill 2338, Talent Protections Act, 2017–18 Reg Sess, California, 2018 § 1700.51.
101 Ibid § 1700.50.
102 Bildfell (n 44) 58.
103 Rachel F Rodgers et al, 'Results of a Strategic Science Study to Inform Policies Targeting Extreme Thinness Standards in the Fashion Industry' (2017) 50(3) *The International Journal of Eating Disorders* 284, 289.
104 Alison Fixsen, Magdalena Kossewska and Aurore Bardey, 'I'm Skinny, I'm Worth More: Fashion Models' Experiences of Aesthetic Labor and Its Impact on Body Image and Eating Behaviors' (2023) 33(1–2) *Qualitative Health Research* 81, 87.
105 Antonio Preti et al, 'Eating Disorders among Professional Fashion Models' (2008) 159(1) *Psychiatry Research* 86, 91–92.
106 Nikolett Bogár et al, 'Frequency of Disordered Eating Habits among Fashion Models' (2022) 30(6) *European Eating Disorders Review* 823, 825, 828.
107 Rodgers et al (n 49) 436.
108 Ibid.

As an added benefit to making models' health a priority, this could result in less thin-ideal images and align with Body Image Law's original aims. One of the limbs of the current Body Image Law assesses models' health, with particular reference to their BMI (France)[109] or requires them to have a minimum BMI (Israel).[110] This limb may benefit the models' health, too, and body image generally (because the public sees less thin-ideal images if models abide by the law). The next issue becomes what other measures should be taken to improve models' health.

For a start, research on the impact on models' health of the Body Image Law limb just discussed would be helpful. It could also be useful to obtain research on how successful the California Law to give nutrition and eating disorder information to models was: whether models read this information and made positive changes that improved their health. If so, then politicians may want to consider passing similar laws or amending their current Body Image Law so that it requires modelling agencies to provide information about nutrition and eating disorders and anything else that is health-related that experts believe may be useful. Nevertheless, it is important to research and further consider how to modify Body Image Law to help improve the health of models.

Types of Body Image Bills That Did Not Pass (Number Three): Banning Thin Models from Catwalks

In the United Kingdom, Caroline Nokes M.P., who led the United Kingdom's All Parliamentary Group on Body Image, campaigned for a law that would not allow thin models to model on catwalks.[111] She contacted academics, health experts, the modelling industry and fashion designers to consult about the law, but members of the modelling industry and fashion industry did not respond.[112]

109 *Code du travail* [Labour Code] (France) art L. 7123-2-1.

110 תעצה קוח תלבגה לקשמ ףנעב תונמגודה [Law for Restricting Weight in the Modelling Industry], 27 March 2012, 5772-2012 ss 1, 2(a).

111 Rebecca Williams, 'Body Image MP Calls For Thin Model Catwalk Ban | UK News | Sky News', *Sky News* (online, 16 September 2015) <https://news.sky.com/story/body-image-mp-calls-for-thin-model-catwalk-ban-10346053>.

112 Tracy McVeigh, 'Why Is a Size-Six Woman Too Big to Model Clothes, Demands Tory MP', *The Observer* (online, 8 November 2015) <https://www.theguardian.com/fashion/2015/nov/08/super-skinny-models-mp-caroline-nokes-ban-debate>.

Types of Body Image Bills That Did Not Pass (Number Four): Bills That Required Collecting Information

American Senator Tammy Baldwin was one of the sponsors of the Healthy Media for Youth Act in 2010 in the United States Federal House of Representatives.[113] Part of the bill states that it would fund education about how images of girls and women in the media can negatively impact youths' body image.[114] It also stated that it would support partnerships that encourage businesses, advertisers, the entertainment industry and other content providers to promote media content that encourages healthy body image.[115] It would also support research on how the media affects body image during child development, among other topics.[116] It further said that the Federal Communications Commission would create the National Task Force on Girls and Women in the Media, to create voluntary guidance to promote 'healthy and positive depictions' of girls and women in the media for young people.[117] This bill did not become law.[118] Senator Baldwin reintroduced the bill at a later date,[119] but again, it did not pass.[120]

In 2014, Representative Ileana Ros-Lehtinen introduced the Truth in Advertising Act in the United States Congress.[121] This bill, if it became law, would have required the Federal Trade Commission ('F.T.C.') to give a report to Congress about how many images in advertisements and other American media included digitally altered models' faces and bodies. The bill also required the F.T.C. to create a strategy to reduce how often people use digitally altered images of models' faces and bodies and recommend a regulatory framework in this area.[122] This bill was unique because it relates to research

113 'Details for H.R. 4925 (111th): Healthy Media for Youth Act', *GovTrack.us* <https://www.govtrack.us/congress/bills/111/hr4925/cosponsors>.

114 Healthy Media for Youth Act, H.R. 4925, 111th Congress, 2010 § 3(a)(2)(D).

115 Ibid § 3(2)(g).

116 Ibid § 4(1)(b).

117 Ibid § 5(a).

118 GovTrack.US, *H.R. 4925 (111th): Healthy Media for Youth Act* (Web Page) <https://govtrack.us/congress/bills/111/hr4925>.

119 Healthy Media for Youth Act, H.R. 2513, 112th Congress (2011); 'Healthy Media for Youth Act (2011); (112th Congress H.R. 2513) – GovTrack.Us', *GovTrack.us* <https://www.govtrack.us/congress/bills/112/hr2513>.

120 'Healthy Media for Youth Act (2011; 112th Congress H.R. 2513) – GovTrack.Us', *GovTrack.us* <https://www.govtrack.us/congress/bills/112/hr2513>.

121 Truth in Advertising Act, H.R.4341, 113th Congress (2014); 'H.R.4341 – 113th Congress (2013-2014): To Direct the Federal Trade Commission to Submit to Congress a Report on the Use, in Advertising and Other Media for the Promotion of Commercial Products, of Images That Have Been Altered to Materially Change the Physical Characteristics of the Faces and Bodies of the Individuals Depicted', *Congress.gov* (29 April 2014) <https://www.congress.gov/bill/113th-congress/house-bill/4341>.

122 Melanie Navamanikkam, 'Truth in Advertising: Should America Ban Photoshop?', *University of Cincinnati Law Review Blog* (Blog Post, 21 June 2017) <https://uclawreview.org/2017

and strategy: it is the only one of its kind in this area of law that the author could find. At the same time, part of the bill was arguably not useful: there may be no point in creating a report that states how many faces and bodies of models were modified when it is common knowledge, and probably sufficient to know, that it is a high number. However, one way that this information could potentially be helpful would be if it was used to see if the number of digitally altered faces and bodies increased or decreased on a regular basis.

This bill related to providing information and strategy only: it had no requirement to act on the information and strategy, though you would hope that businesses might decide to act of their own volition. Since there was no requirement to act on the information and strategy, it is possible that no direct measures would have been taken to reduce the number of thin-ideal images that the public sees had the bill become law, which it did not.[123] When it was re-introduced in Congress in 2016 it did not pass.[124]

Types of Body Image Bills That Did Not Pass (Number Five): Bills That Proposed Taxes

'A tax credit is a dollar-for-dollar amount taxpayers claim on their tax return to reduce the income tax they owe. Eligible taxpayers can use them to reduce their tax bill and potentially increase their refund'.[125] In Massachusetts, United States, Kay Khan, from the State's House of Representatives, introduced a bill that would have provided tax credits to businesses that did not alter images of models' body size, body shape, skin tone and skin texture (including wrinkles).[126] The tax credit would have been the equivalent to 1% of the cost of purchases associated with an advertising campaign. The total could not exceed

/06/21/truth-in-advertising-should-america-ban-photoshop/>; Truth in Advertising Act, H.R. 4341, 113th Congress (2014).

123 Truth in Advertising Act, H.R. 4341, 113th Congress (2014).

124 Elisa S Danthinne et al, 'Beauty and the Big Business: A Qualitative Investigation of the Development and Implementation of the CVS Beauty Mark' (2022) 41 *Body Image* 74, 78; Melanie Navamanikkam, 'Truth in Advertising: Should America Ban Photoshop?', *University of Cincinnati Law Review Blog* (21 June 2017) <https://uclawreview.org/2017/06/21/truth-in-advertising-should-america-ban-photoshop/>; Truth in Advertising Act, H.R.4341, 113th Congress (2014); 'H.R.4341 – 113th Congress (2013-2014): To Direct the Federal Trade Commission to Submit to Congress a Report on the Use, in Advertising and Other Media for the Promotion of Commercial Products, of Images That Have Been Altered to Materially Change the Physical Characteristics of the Faces and Bodies of the Individuals Depicted', *Congress.gov* (29 April 2014) <https://www.congress.gov/bill/113th-congress/house-bill/4341>.

125 Internal Revenue Service, 'Tax Credits for Individuals: What They Mean and How They Can Help Refunds' (Web Page, April 2023) <https://www.irs.gov/newsroom/tax-credits-for-individuals-what-they-mean-and-how-they-can-help-refunds>.

126 Commonwealth of Massachusetts, An Act Relative to Mental Health Promotion through Realistic Advertising Images, House Bill H 2860, § 1.

$10,000 in any tax year.[127] The bill was referred to the Committee on Revenue in June 2019 and sent for a study order in February 2020. It did not become law.[128] This was the first time a tax credit involving body image was introduced in the United States[129] or the world (as far as the author is aware). 'This bill will hopefully spur companies to lean into the body confidence movement and realize that consumers would like to see themselves – their real selves – in the media', said Ms Khan.[130] From a practical perspective, this bill appears to make sense, since it is possible to use technology to learn the amount that an image was digitally altered to help enforce it.[131] STRIPED supported the bill.[132]

This bill is important, because it is one of the few pieces of legislation in the Body Image Law area that used a carrot (as opposed to a stick) approach: it involved rewarding businesses for practices that may contribute to positive body image, instead of punishing them. It is contentious whether a maximum of $10,000 is an appropriate amount for the tax credit. Perhaps it would have been more appropriate to give tax credits that are a percentage of revenue: this way the actual amount that a business would have to pay would be more relevant to the actual business. If passed, the bill could have caused the Massachusetts Government to lose tax revenue, though it could have possibly not had to spend as much money to treat eating disorders, if it had resulted in people in the State seeing less images of the thin-ideal and less people in the State having eating disorders. Nevertheless, trying to improve the health of people who live in Massachusetts should be more important than financial matters.

Government and Industry Policies That Appear Similar to Body Image Laws

This section will discuss the efforts of the Quebec Government, the Government of London, England, the British Fashion Council, fashion week organisers in Milan and Madrid, the Council of Fashion Designers of America and various businesses to create policies that are similar in content and/or spirit to Body Image Law.

The Provincial Government in Quebec, Canada, created the Quebec Charter for a Healthy and Diverse Body Image ('Charter') in 2012. The

127 Ibid.

128 The General Court of the Commonwealth of Massachusetts, *Bill H.3892*, <https://malegislature.gov/Bills/191/HD2881> (last visited Jun 12, 2021).

129 Amani Mansour, Todd Datz and Tamara Sobel, 'Chairwoman Kay Khan Targets Advertisers with #theRealMe Bill: New Legislation Incentivizes Companies to Use Unedited Images of Models' (Press Release, Massachusetts House of Representatives, 30 May 2019) <https://hsph.harvard.edu/wp content/uploads/2024/11/Press-Release-Digitally-Altered-Ads.pdf>.

130 Ibid.

131 Eric Kee and Hany Farid, 'Perceptual Metric for Photo Retouching' (2011) 108(50) *Proceedings of the National Academy of Sciences – PNAS* 19907, 19907, 19909.

132 Mansour, Datz and Sobel (n 129).

Quebec Minister of Communication, Culture and the Status of Women requested its creation in 2009[133] and the Quebec Government organised a taskforce to construct it.[134] The Charter states actions that people and organisations can take to change society to try to lessen pressure to have a thin body. Following the Charter is voluntary and the Quebec Government encouraged fashion and media industries to implement it. The Charter urged people to

> pledge to 1. promote a diversity of body images, including different heights, proportions, and ages; 2. encourage healthy eating and weight-control habits; 3. discourage excessive weight-control practices or appearance modification; 4. refuse to subscribe to esthetic ideals based on extreme thinness; 5. remain vigilant and diligent so as to minimize the risks of anorexia nervosa, bulimia nervosa, and unhealthy preoccupations with weight; 6. act as agents of change so as to promote healthy eating and weight-control practices and realistic body images; and 7. promote the Québec Charter for a Healthy and Diverse Body Image among partners, clients, and others while actively respecting and adhering to its principles.[135]

The Quebec Charter was promoted at various events, and did not receive much overall publicity.[136]

A survey of 1,003 people in Quebec six months after the Charter was launched found that 35% of survey participants had heard about it.[137] Women and highly educated people were more likely to know about the Charter.[138] About 33% of survey participants thought that the Charter 'had high potential to sensitize people in the population to issues of body image and disordered eating, but only about 14% reported that potential actions proposed in it had high potential to reduce sociocultural pressures favoring thinness'.[139]

Another study on the Charter, published in 2018, involved 2,180 Quebec adults who responded to an online survey to consider their body dissatisfaction and thoughts towards the Charter.[140] The researchers found that people

133 Farah Islam, 'Promoting Healthy Body Images in Populations: Does Body Dissatisfaction Influence Reactions to Quebec's Charter for Healthy and Diverse Body Image?' (Masters Thesis, Université de Montreal, 2018) 1.

134 Ibid.

135 Lise Gauvin and Howard Steiger, 'Overcoming the Unhealthy Pursuit of Thinness: Reaction to the Québec Charter for a Healthy and Diverse Body Image' (2012) 102(8) *American Journal of Public Health* 1600, 1600.

136 Susan J Paxton, 'Social Policy and Prevention' in Michael P Levine and Linda Smola (eds), *The Wiley Handbook of Eating Disorders* (John Wiley & Sons, Ltd, 2015) 663.

137 Gauvin and Steiger (n 135) 1604.

138 Ibid 1605.

139 Ibid 603.

140 Islam (n 133) 24.

who wanted to lose weight were more likely to support the Charter than those who did not.[141]

Neither of these research studies, nor any research study that the author could find, examined whether creating the Charter resulted in less thin-ideal images in Quebec advertising, and in turn, how that impacted body image and eating disorders. This information would be useful to assess whether the Charter had a practical positive impact, rather than merely resulting in increasing awareness of body image, eating disorders and the effects of seeing thin-ideal images. In fact, addressing poor body image and lowering the number of people who have eating disorders is the aim of Body Image Law, not increasing awareness (though increasing awareness of these issues is, nevertheless, an important step in that process).

The Australian Government appointed a National Advisory Group on Body Image in 2009, which created a Voluntary Industry Code of Conduct on Body Image ('Code'). The Code gives guidance on body image 'to build on and further encourage the positive steps that are taken within the fashion, media and advertising industries to bring about long-term cultural change'.[142]

The Code states principles to help industries undertake more measures that can help body image.[143] Specifically, it states that advertisers should use models who are 'a healthy weight and shape'.[144] The document does not state what a 'healthy weight' is.[145] Instead, it recommends consulting websites like www.healthyactive.gov.au/healthyweight and www.nhmrc.gov.au and people in the health profession should obtain guidance on this. It also says that people who hire models should think about their models' health and take action to become satisfied that models are healthy before hiring them. It encourages using models who are a diverse range of sizes, shapes and ethnicities. It further says that people should not use digital technology to modify images so that models' body shape and features look unrealistic or unattainable through healthy behaviour, and when images are modified it should be brought to viewers' attention.[146]

In contrast to the Quebec Charter, there is some research that examined how the Code impacted the quantity of images containing the thin-ideal in Australia. In 2010, a year after the Code was passed, researchers implemented a qualitative content analysis of 10 Australian swimsuit magazines for young women to see if they implemented the Code. Only one of the 10 magazines

141 Ibid 28.

142 Australian Government, 'Voluntary Industry Code of Conduct on Body Image' (Web Page) <http://www.mediaknite.org/wp-content/uploads/2016/07/Body-Image-code-of-conduct.pdf>.

143 Ibid.

144 Ibid.

145 Ibid.

146 Ibid.

fully implemented it,[147] though the majority of the magazines implemented part of it and most of the magazines that they considered followed important parts of the Code by having models with diverse body sizes.[148] The researchers wrote that the Code did not address words that could negatively impact body image that the articles used, like stating ways to hide 'lumps' and 'bumps'.[149] It added that while the magazines contained diverse-sized models, they did not replace thin models.[150]

Another Australian study, undertaken five years after the Code was released, examined whether 13 Australian magazines adopted the Code.[151] The study found that

> [o]verall there was little diversity amongst body images represented in Australian women's fashion magazines. Across the 13 magazines examined, models were mostly underweight, white and young. Just 1 in 4 models were observed to be of an appropriate weight or larger, with less than 1% discerned to be overweight. There was little difference in diversity between advertisements and non-advertisements aside from a small representation of overweight body sizes in the non-advertisement images.[152]

It further stated that this is

> disappointing given recent efforts to change practices and improve diversity in the representation of females in the media. Unfortunately, these findings appear to confirm that voluntary efforts such as the Australian Voluntary Industry Code of Conduct on Body Image have had no more than a placatory and short-lived impact on media practices, at least in the print media. Initiatives by government, industry and other sectors are to be commended, yet there is a clear need to ensure these initiatives are effectively implemented and evaluated in an ongoing manner to ensure sustained impact.[153]

147 Elizabeth Reid Boyd and Jessica Moncrieff-Boyd, 'Swimsuit Issues: Promoting Positive Body Image in Young Women's Magazines' (2011) 22(2) *Health Promotion Journal of Australia* 102, 104.

148 Ibid 104–105.

149 Ibid 105.

150 Ibid.

151 Catarina de Freitas, Helen Jordan and Elizabeth K Hughes, 'Body Image Diversity in the Media: A Content Analysis of Women's Fashion Magazines' (2018) 29(3) *Health Promotion Journal of Australia* 251, 253.

152 Ibid 253.

153 Ibid 254.

The Danish Fashion Institute created the Danish Fashion Ethical Charter in 2007 ('Charter') with the Danish Association against Eating Disorders and Self-Harm. It has been updated a few times since its creation. The Charter states that fashion companies, photographers, advertising agencies, etc. must give models healthy and nutritious food when they work for more than two hours. It further states that in 2017 the steering committee of the Charter undertook a pilot programme with 16-year-old and some 15-year-old models, which involved giving models health checks. This consisted of interviewing models using the Eating Disorder Examination (a tool to diagnose eating disorders) which lasts for approximately 90 minutes. The assessment considered whether a model may be at risk of an eating disorder or potentially has one. If it appears likely that a model has an eating disorder, they are told to see their doctor and cannot work again until they are 'cleared'.[154] Every time a model has a health check, their visit is recorded and the Danish Association against Eating Disorders and Self-Harm informs their agency. In 2019 and onward they wanted to include 16-, 18- and 20-year-old models and models for whom they are concerned about their behaviour or body measurements in the health check.[155] The Charter's website has a list of over 300 brands, modelling agencies, photographers, stores, etc. that signed it.[156] If a signatory to the Charter does not follow it, then their name can appear on the 'Blacklist' webpage for the Charter.[157] Danish designers must sign the Charter to participate in Danish Fashion Week.[158] Since part of Body Image Law involves requiring models to be healthy to work, and the author proposed that Body Image Law starts to encompass improving models' health as a priority, it would be helpful to learn the outcome of this initiative: the impact that it had on models' health and the body image of the Danish people. The author could not find any research on it.

Transport for London is a local government body responsible for managing all public transport in London, and its main roads.[159] The organisation changed its advertising policy in 2016 so that it does not allow advertisements on its buses and other vehicles that 'could reasonably be seen as likely to cause pressure to conform to an unrealistic or unhealthy body shape, or as

154 *Danish Fashion Ethical Charter* (Web Page) <http://danishfashionethicalcharter.com/>.

155 Ibid.

156 'Signatories', *Danish Fashion Ethical Charter* (Web Page) <http://danishfashionethicalcharter.com/underskrivere/>.

157 'Black List', *Danish Fashion Ethical Charter* (Web Page) <http://danishfashionethicalcharter.com/black-list/>.

158 Namrata Bhowmik and Naman Anand, 'From Models to Mannequins: The Oxymoronic Equation of International Labor Law Standards in the World of Fashion' (2023) 71 *Cleveland State Law Review* 811, 840.

159 Transport for London, 'What We Do' (Web Page) <https://www.tfl.gov.uk/corporate/about-tfl/what-we-do>.

likely to create body confidence issues particularly among young people'.[160] Like other policies related to body image that this book discusses, its wording is vague, which can make implementing it difficult. Transport for London's application of this policy did not negatively impact its revenue, which supports the idea that advertising that tries to improve body image does not affect profits.[161] The author could not find any research regarding how many thin-ideal images were present before Transport for London implemented the policy and after, and what percentage of images out of a total number of images that a person in London would be likely to see are on public transportation. This information would help to give an idea of the impact that this initiative might have.

In the United Kingdom, the British Fashion Council, a not-for-profit organisation, held a Model Health Inquiry which involved people in the fashion industry and people who worked in eating disorders proposing recommendations to try to support the health of models in the fashion industry.[162] The Inquiry's report suggested that models who participate in London Fashion Week must give a medical certificate from a doctor who has experience in recognising eating disorders that states that they are in 'good health' so they can work.[163] Models would need to organise and pay for their own medical appointments to obtain certificates. They also recommended that all models who participate in London Fashion Week must be hired through modelling agencies based in the United Kingdom to enforce the health checks.[164] It additionally suggested creating a voluntary code concerning digitally modifying models' images.[165] In 2008, a pilot programme which required models who participated in London Fashion Week to provide health certificates occurred. Most models resisted being part of it.[166] They felt that it took significant time, was expensive and the health checks were impractical or ineffective.[167]

Similarly, in a research study, researchers asked models about different potential initiatives to lessen the pressure they experience to match the

160 'Tfl Advertising Policy' (25 February 2019) <https://content.tfl.gov.uk/tfl-advertising-policy-250219.pdf>.

161 Evidence to House of Commons, Women and Equalities Committee (Parliament of the United Kingdom, 2 December 2020, Centre for Appearance Research) <https://committees.parliament.uk/oralevidence/1410/pdf>.

162 British Fashion Council, *Fashioning a Healthy Future The Report of the Model Health Inquiry* (Report, September 2007) 1–2 <https://www.britishfashioncouncil.co.uk/uploads/files/1/The%20Report%20of%20the%20Model%20Health%20Inquiry,%20September%202007.pdf>.

163 Ibid 4.

164 Ibid 6.

165 Ibid.

166 British Fashion Council, *Review of Model Health Inquiry Recommendations and Opportunities* (Report, February 2016) <https://www.britishfashioncouncil.co.uk/uploads/files/1/Model%20Health%20Inquiry%20Review%20Feb%2016.pdf>.

167 Ibid.

thin-ideal. Models did not support policy that required a minimum BMI to work, because they thought it was unlikely to have a good result and would be hard to implement. They preferred giving models better employment conditions, such as meals and breaks. A potential reason why models did not support a requirement to have a minimum BMI to work is because they may support the thin-ideal.[168]

The models' reaction is significant. If models don't support a Body Image Law initiative, then they may be less likely to abide by it, even if it means breaching the law. This is particularly the case if only employers of models are responsible for any negative legal consequences resulting from breaching the law and not the models themselves, though the author does not suggest holding the models responsible. It may be that an education programme teaching models about the reasons for Body Image Law and the connection between seeing thin-ideal images and developing poor body image could help to gain models' support for a Body Image Law. It is important to introduce practical ways to address models' lack of support for Body Image Law, if the law's effectiveness is to be increased.

In 2006, a trade association, the Spanish Association of Fashion Designers,[169] forbade models with a BMI under 18 from participating in the Madrid Fashion Week.[170] The Madrid Government sponsored the show and Madrid Regional Official Concha Guerra said '[f]ashion is a mirror and many teenagers imitate what they see on the catwalk'.[171]

There were reports of the ban being implemented: in its first year, about 30% of models were not allowed to participate in Madrid Fashion Week[172] for being too thin.[173] There were anecdotal reports that some models cheated to appear to have an appropriate BMI: they wore Spanx with weighted sandbags and put weights in their hair.[174] They instituted this ban after Luisel Ramos, a Uruguayan supermodel, died due to complications from Anorexia Nervosa,

168 Rodgers et al (n 103) 290.
169 Bhowmik and Anand (n 158) 847.
170 'Madrid Bans Waifs from Catwalks', *BBC News* (online, 13 September 2006) <http://news.bbc.co.uk/2/hi/5341202.stm>.
171 'Skinny Models Banned', *Sydney Morning Herald* (online, 13 September 2006) <https://www.smh.com.au/lifestyle/fashion/skinny-models-banned-20060913-gdodrf.html>.
172 Selina Sykes, 'Six Countries Taking Steps to Tackle Super-Skinny Models', *euronews* (online, 6 September 2017) <https://www.euronews.com/2017/09/06/counties-fighting-underweight-modelling>.
173 'Super-Thin Models: Controversy Grows', *CBS News* (online, 18 September 2006) <https://www.cbsnews.com/news/super-thin-models-controversy-grows/>.
174 Jennifer Sky, 'Are Models Being Forced Into Extreme Measures to Conceal Their Weight?', *Observer* (online, 21 April 2015) <https://observer.com/2015/04/young-models-are-not-to-blame-for-industry-pressure-to-be-thin/>

soon after she finished modelling in a runway fashion show.[175] This was the first ban internationally of thin models from walking at fashion shows.[176] The fashion industry opposed the ban: Cathy Gould, from New York's Elite Modeling Agency, said that the fashion industry was a 'scapegoat' for eating disorders.[177] A better way of looking at this issue may be that the fashion industry is part of the problem, and trying to lower the number of thin-ideal models who participate in fashion shows is one way to try to address it.

Not long after the Madrid ban, Brazilian supermodel Ana Carolina Restona also died from an illness caused by Anorexia Nervosa.[178] The supermodel deaths caused Milan to follow Madrid's lead and banned models with a BMI under 18.5 from walking in runway shows.[179] In 2012, the Council of Fashion Designers of America released new guidelines related to models' health. They stated that models had to be at least aged 16 to walk on runways. Models under 18 should not walk past midnight and their identification should be checked. Models who may have an eating disorder should be encouraged to obtain professional help and models receiving professional help should not continue to model without the approval of the person who provides them with professional help.[180]

Individual businesses also took action that appears to be similar in spirit to Body Image Law, on their own volition: no law required them to. In 2007, international company Unilever decided not to use 'size zero' models or actors in its advertising.[181] They also expected their staff to use models and actors with a BMI roughly between 18.5 and 25, since this applies the World Health Organization's guideline on a healthy BMI.[182] The author could not find evidence regarding whether this policy was implemented. The staff of one of Unilever's brands, Dove (a soap), runs the Dove Self-Esteem Project, which tries to improve self-esteem and offers resources to help do so.[183] Dove

175 Galya Hildesheimer and Hemda Gur-Arie, 'Just Modeling? The Modeling Industry, Eating Disorders, and the Law' (2015) 8(2) *International Journal of Feminist Approaches to Bioethics* 103, 105.

176 'Skinny Models Banned' (ibid 171).

177 Ibid.

178 Hildesheimer and Gur-Arie (n 175) 105.

179 'Milan Bans Ultra-Skinny Models from Catwalk', *Reuters* (online, 9 August 2007) <https://www.reuters.com/article/world/milan-bans-ultra-skinny-models-from-catwalk-idUSL19249915/>.

180 Ellie Krupnick, 'CFDA Announces Latest Runway Health Guidelines', *HuffPost* (online, 27 January 2012) <https://www.huffpost.com/entry/cfda-health-guidelines-for-models_n_1236213>.

181 'Advertising and Marketing', *Unilever* (Web Page) <https://www.unilever.com/sustainability/responsible-business/advertising-and-marketing/>.

182 Ibid; W.H.O., *A Healthy Lifestyle, WHO Recommendations* (Web Page, 6 May 2010) <https://www.who.int/europe/news-room/fact-sheets/item/a-healthy-lifestyle---who-recommendations>.

183 Unilever, 'The Dove Self-Esteem Project', *Dove* (Web Page) <https://www.dove.com/au/dove-self-esteem-project.html>.

also has a 'real beauty pledge', which involves using typical women, instead of models, in their advertising.[184]

Representatives of Getty Images, the largest stock photo agency internationally, stated in 2017 that they would not accept images of models whose bodies were modified to be smaller or larger.[185] The staff of Sport England, Boohoo, Dove and L'Oréal stated they do not digitally modify the images that they use in their advertising,[186] and Target released a swimsuit campaign with images of models that were not retouched.[187]

Staff of LVMH and Kering, two of the world's biggest fashion houses, responsible for brands Christian Dior, Givenchy, Yves Saint Laurent, Alexander McQueen, Marc Jacobs and Gucci, stated that they would not use underweight models for their fashion shows.[188] They added that their models must have bodies larger than a French size 32, which is about a U.S. size zero and they would not use models under age 16 to wear adult clothes.[189] Kering's Chairman, François-Henri Pinault, stated that he hoped that the rest of the industry would follow its lead.[190]

Staff of CVS, a large American pharmacy chain, decided in 2018 not to alter the models in their advertising in several ways, such as not changing their shape, size and proportion.[191] They also created the 'CVS Beauty Mark' to add to images that were not significantly modified.[192] Further, they worked with about 600 influencers to share over 500 social media images that were not altered.[193] CVS staff believed this campaign would make them a leader.[194] The 'CVS Beauty Mark' was well received, thought to be innovative and to inspire change,[195] and it was meant to increase the number of its millennial

184 Dove, 'Real Beauty Pledge' (Web Page) <https://www.dove.com/au/stories/about-dove/dove-real-beauty-pledge.html>.

185 Steve Dent, 'Getty Bans Images Photoshopped to Make Models Look Thinner', *Engadget* (online, 27 September 2017) <https://www.engadget.com/2017-09-27-getty-bans-photoshop-images-models-thinner.html>.

186 House of Commons, Women and Equalities, *Changing the Perfect Picture: An Inquiry into Body Image* (Report No HC 274, 9 April 2021) <https://committees.parliament.uk/publications/5357/documents/53751/default/>.

187 Jeff Beer, 'Target's 2018 Swimwear Campaign Features Photoshop-Free Models', *Fast Company* (online, 19 March 2018) <https://www.fastcompany.com/40546177/targets-2018-swimwear-campaign-features-photoshop-free-models/>.

188 'Christian Dior and Gucci Owners Drop Super-Skinny Models', *BBC News* (online, 6 September 2017) <https://www.bbc.com/news/business-41174739>.

189 Ibid.

190 Ibid.

191 'CVS Beauty Mark', *CVSHealth* (Web Page, 15 October 2021) <https://www.cvshealth.com/news/innovation/cvs-beauty-mark.html>.

192 Ibid.

193 Ibid.

194 Danthinne et al (n 124) 82.

195 Ibid.

consumers.[196] The Truth in Advertising Act (a bill that did not become law, described earlier in this book) inspired CVS staff to create the 'CVS Beauty Mark':[197] they decided to try to improve body image because the bill did not become law.[198]

In terms of the policy, the author could not find any evidence at this point in time that any of the policies discussed are helping body image and/or contributing to lowering the number of thin-ideal images in existence.

In terms of businesses, the number the author could find that made these changes is currently small, and there is little evidence about their impact on body image and eating disorders. The small amount of evidence about these initiatives, such as that concerning the Aerie real campaign, shows that they can be positive for body image.[199]

If, in the future, there is a significant amount of evidence that policy and business initiatives are positive for body image and/or they lower the number of thin-ideal images, then it is worth revisiting the question of whether Body Image Law is needed to try to improve body image.

Self-Regulation in Advertising Industries That Is Similar to Body Image Law

Self-regulation exists in different forms, but essentially it involves an industry voluntarily creating rules for itself that advertisers should follow, but the law does not require them to.[200] Self-regulation is typically more flexible and quicker to introduce than law, which can be a great benefit.[201]

The advertising industry in a few jurisdictions self-regulates on many issues, such as trying to prevent the public from seeing misleading advertising[202] or violence in advertising (unless necessary).[203] Canada,[204] the United Kingdom,[205] Australia[206] and New Zealand[207] all have independent advertising

196 Ibid 78.
197 Ibid.
198 Ibid.
199 Alexandra D Convertino et al, 'An Evaluation of the Aerie Real Campaign: Potential for Promoting Positive Body Image?' (2019) 24(6) *Journal of Health Psychology* 726, 734.
200 Attrill (n 4) 24.
201 Ibid 24–25.
202 See e.g., Advertising Standards Authority (U.K.) and Committee of Advertising Practice (U.K.), '03 Misleading Advertising' (Web Page) <https://www.asa.org.uk/type/non_broadcast/code_section/03.html>.
203 See e.g., Australian Association of National Advertisers, 'Code of Ethics', *AANA* (Web Page) <https://aana.com.au/self-regulation/codes-guidelines/code-of-ethics/>.
204 Ad Standards (Canada), 'Ad Standards–Canada' (Web Page) <https://adstandards.ca/>.
205 A.S.A., 'About ASA and CAP' (Web Page) <https://www.asa.org.uk/about-asa-and-cap.html>.
206 Australian Association of National Advertisers, 'A.A.N.A.' (Web Page) <https://aana.com.au/>.
207 Advertising Standards Authority, 'About Us' (Web Page) <https://asa.co.nz/about-us/>.

regulators that create the standard for advertisers to follow in their respective jurisdictions. Each of those regulators produced written codes for advertisers to follow.[208]

The code of ethics (or a similar document) that these organisations created directly mentions body image-related issues,[209] with the exception of Canada's.[210] As a result, the rest of this section will exclusively discuss the advertising self-regulation in the United Kingdom, Australia and New Zealand.

There are different, though similar, consequences in each of the three jurisdictions if an advertiser breached an advertising code. In the United Kingdom, the Advertising Standards Authority ('A.S.A.') is the independent advertising regulator responsible for ensuring that U.K. advertisements do not breach the U.K. Advertising Codes. The Committee of Advertising Practice ('C.A.P.') is a sister organisation of A.S.A. and writes the Advertising Codes.[211] Anyone can complain to the A.S.A. about an advertisement within three months after an advertisement appeared.[212] If a business does not comply with an A.S.A. ruling, it can damage their reputation,[213] and some of the main actions that A.S.A. staff can take against an advertiser that it decided breached the codes are: add the business' name and information about the problem with their advertising to a specific section of the A.S.A. website until the advertiser complies, ask search engines to remove paid-search advertisements that contain a link to the material that breached the rules and work with social media companies to remove the material from their platforms.[214]

208 A.A.N.A., 'Code of Ethics' (Web Page, February 2001) <https://f.hubspotusercontent00.net/hubfs/5093205/AANA_Code_of_Ethics_Effective_February_2021.pdf?utm_campaign=Self-Reg-Codes&utm_source=AANA&utm_medium=web&utm_term=self-reg&utm_content=code-of-ethics>; A.S.A., 'Advertising Standards Code' (Web Page) <https://asa.co.nz/wp-content/uploads/2025/04/ASA-Advertising-Standards-Code-April-2025.pdf>; Ad Standards, 'The Canadian Code of Advertising Standards' (Web Page, July 2019) <https://adstandards.ca/code/the-code-online/>; A.S.A., 'Advertising Standards Code' (Web Page) <ASA-Advertising-Standards-Code-April-2025.pdf>.

209 A.S.A., 'About ASA and CAP' (Web Page) <https://www.asa.org.uk/about-asa-and-cap.html>; 'Australian Association of National Advertisers' (Web Page) <https://aana.com.au/>; Advertising Standards Authority, 'About Us' (Web Page) <https://asa.co.nz/about-us/>.

210 The author checked on 11 March 2025, and the Canadian Code of Advertising Standards did not have any Clauses that directly mentioned eating disorders: <https://adstandards.ca/code/the-code-online/>.

211 Advertising Standards Authority (U.K.) and Committee of Advertising Practice (U.K.), 'About the ASA and CAP' (Web Page) <https://www.asa.org.uk/about-asa-and-cap/about-regulation/about-the-asa-and-cap.html>.

212 'Marketing and Advertising: The Law', *GOV.UK* (Web Page) <https://www.gov.uk/marketing-advertising-law/advertising-codes-of-practice>.

213 Advertising Standards Authority (U.K.) and Committee of Advertising Practice (U.K.), 'Sanctions' (Web Page) <https://www.asa.org.uk/codes-and-rulings/sanctions.html>.

214 Ibid.

In Australia, the Australian Association of National Advertisers ('A.A.N.A.')[215] is the organisation that creates, reviews and updates the codes that regulate Australian advertisers. Ad Standards is an independent Australian organisation that investigates and deals with complaints the public makes regarding breaches of the advertising codes that A.A.N.A. made. Ad Standards has a Community Panel, an independent, impartial group with people from different ages and backgrounds, who do not work in advertising, who decide on the Panel's behalf whether an advertisement breached one of A.A.N.A.'s Codes. Ad Standards typically receives over 3,000 complaints and investigates hundreds of advertisements per year. All of the Community Panel's decisions are published on the Ad Standards website.[216] If an advertiser does not abide by a Community Panel decision, the Ad Standards website states that it will try enforcement options, such as contacting the owner of the media that published the advertisement to ask them to remove it.[217] The website does not list other specific actions that Ad Standards takes when an advertiser does not abide by a Community Panel decision.[218]

The Advertising Standards Authority is New Zealand's advertising self-regulating body.[219] It creates standards for advertising, and consumers can contact the organisation to complain about advertisements.[220] If the organisation decides that a complaint is valid, then it will ask for the advertisement to be removed.[221]

The U.K. Advertising Standards Authority, the Australian Association of National Advertisers and the New Zealand Advertising Standards Authority all have a written code or resources that contain a small part relating to body image. An A.S.A. resource for advertisers, *Social Responsibility: Body Image*, states,

> [a]dvertisers should ensure that they don't portray particular body types in an irresponsible manner or present an unhealthy body image as aspirational, exploit people's insecurities about their body image, or suggest that happiness or wellbeing depends on conforming to a particular physical

215 Australian Association of National Advertisers, 'Our History', *AANA* (Web Page, 2024) <https://aana.com.au/about-us/our-history/>.

216 Australian Association of National Advertisers, 'About', *AANA* (Web Page) <https://aana.com.au/about-us/>; Ad Standards, 'Community Panel' (Web Page) <https://adstandards.com.au/about/community-panel/>.

217 Ad Standards, 'The Advertising Complaints Process' (Web Page) <https://adstandards.com.au/about/advertising-complaints-process/>.

218 Ibid.

219 Advertising Standards Authority (N.Z.), 'About Us' (Web Page, 25 November 2024) <https://asa.co.nz/about-us/>.

220 Ibid.

221 Ad Standards, 'The Advertising Complaints Process' (Web Page) <https://adstandards.com.au/about/advertising-complaints-process/>.

appearance, or gender stereotypical body type or physical features (rule 4.9).[222]

The resource also says that '[a]dvertisers must ensure that models are not depicted in a way which makes them appear underweight or unhealthy, as this could be considered irresponsible for promoting an unhealthy body image'.[223] It further maintains that advertisements should not imply that people will be happy once they or their body looks a certain way.[224]

Section 2.6 of the A.A.N.A.'s *Code of Ethics* states that '[a]dvertising shall not depict material contrary to Prevailing Community Standards on health and safety'.[225] The New Zealand Advertising Standards Authority's *Children's Advertising Code* states that 'advertising must not provide an unrealistic sense of body image or promote an unhealthy lifestyle or create undue pressure to conform'.[226] It adds that 'this includes the denigration of healthy lifestyles, depiction or encouragement of unhealthy lifestyles and pressure to conform to a particular body image'.[227]

The author searched the online database of decisions for the three organisations to learn how they adjudicated decisions that allegedly breached their respective codes that dealt with body image. Annexure B in this book contains a list of all the decisions that she found. Twenty-one cases came before the U.K. Advertising Standards Authority: they upheld 18 fully and one in part.[228] Two decisions came before the Australian Community Panel: they did not uphold either.[229] Four decisions came before the New Zealand Advertising Standards Authority: it did not uphold any of the decisions, but in two of the decisions the advertiser modified or removed

222 Advertising Standards Authority (U.K.) and Committee of Advertising Practice, 'Social Responsibility: Body Image' (Web Page, 12 February 2025) <https://www.asa.org.uk/advice-online/social-responsibility-body-image.html>.

223 Ibid.

224 Ibid.

225 Australian Association of National Advertisers, 'Code of Ethics', *AANA* <https://aana.com.au/self-regulation/codes-guidelines/code-of-ethics/>.

226 Advertising Standards Authority (N.Z.), 'Children's Advertising Code' 19 January 2025 <https://asa.co.nz/codes/codes/childrens-advertising-code/>.

227 Ibid.

228 On 28 April 2025 the author visited the website, <https://www.asa.org.uk/codes-and-rulings/rulings.html>. In the section at the top of the page, 'search rulings', the author entered the phrase 'body image'. Eighteen decisions were upheld, two were not upheld and one was upheld in part.

229 On 28 April 2025 the author visited the website, <https://adstandards.com.au/cases/>. In the section titled 'Code', there was a dropdown menu. She chose the option 'AANA Code of Ethics'. Another dropdown menu appeared with different sections of the *Code of Ethics* listed. The author chose the option '2.6 Health and Safety'. Then, another dropdown menu appeared with different topics. The author chose the option 'body image'. Two rulings appeared: the Community Panel dismissed both of those complaints.

the advertisements in question after a complaint was made but before a ruling was handed down.[230]

Body image experts wrote submissions to the U.K. Parliament's Body Image Inquiry in which they stated that they did not believe that models' weights had changed in the previous 10 years, so the A.S.A. was ineffective to regulate body image.[231] Many harmful advertisements, it was said, 'go unnoticed' by the A.S.A. and 'the efficacy of self-regulation as a substitute to statutory control is naïve'.[232]

A better way of approaching this issue may be that self-regulation should not be a substitute to legislation: it should be an addition to it and it has some benefits. A significant benefit of the ability to make complaints to the self-regulatory advertising bodies is that they can empower the members of the public who may feel helpless about the ubiquitous nature of thin-ideal advertisements. Allowing them to complain to an organisation when they see advertisements containing the thin-ideal may give them a sort of agency: they can try to take some action against an advertiser using thin-ideal images. Also, simply knowing about the advertising self-regulation may genuinely deter some advertisers from employing thin-ideal models.

That there are so few decisions that come before the advertising self-regulators supports the argument that they should not be a substitute for effective legislation. The author notes that the number of cases that she found from the advertising self-regulators should be viewed as an estimate since it is possible that if she had used different words or phrases in some of the search engines on their websites, e.g. also searching with the phrase 'body dissatisfaction', she may have found additional cases.

It is important to consider, though, that the decisions that the advertising bodies made related to whether the advertisements breached the advertising codes, and not generally whether the images that they adjudicated actually featured the thin-ideal or could result in harming the body image of the people who viewed them.

On the other hand, some of the decisions of these self-regulatory bodies can receive considerable publicity,[233] and this may itself increase awareness

230 On 28 April 2025 the author visited the website, <https://asa.co.nz/decisions/search-browse-decisions/>. In the box titled 'keyword' the author entered the words 'body image'. Four rulings appeared: in one decision it was decided that there was no jurisdiction to decide the matter, a second decision was not upheld and the remaining two decisions involved the advertiser removing or amending the advertisements after the complaint was made, but before a ruling was handed down.

231 Evidence to House of Commons, Women and Equalities Committee (Parliament of the United Kingdom, 2 December 2020, Lynda Boothroyd, Elizabeth Evans and Katy Jacques) <https://committees.parliament.uk/writtenevidence/7571/pdf/>.

232 Bhowmik and Anand (n 158) 836–837.

233 See, for example, Haroon Siddique, 'Yves Saint Laurent Ad Banned for Using "Unhealthily Underweight" Model', *The Guardian* (online, 2 June 2015) <https://www.theguardian.com/

about the dangers of the thin-ideal. Moreover, somewhat paradoxically, while advertising industry self-regulation is not causing widespread change to the issues that Body Image Law tries to address,[234] it has partially resulted in demand to pass Body Image Law.[235]

Conclusion

This chapter explained the Body Image Laws in detail: they comprise laws passed in Israel, France and Norway, bills introduced in Parliaments in Canada, the United Kingdom, Brazil and the United States and policy and advertising self-regulation in Australia, Spain, Canada, Denmark, Italy and the United Kingdom. On the surface, they may sound like a practical, feasible way to help lower the number of thin-ideal images and lessen the number of people with poor body image and eating disorders. The next chapter will consider this thought, by discussing the challenges associated with the Body Image Law (there are many).

media/2015/jun/03/yves-saint- laurent-ad-ban-underweight-model>; '"Unhealthily Underweight Model" Yves Saint Laurent Advert Banned', *BBC News* (online, 3 June 2015) <https://www.bbc.com/news/uk-32987228>.

234 Attrill (n 4) 19.

235 Ibid 24.

6 Challenges Associated with Body Image Law

Introduction

There are several challenges associated with Body Image Law (in its current form); consequently, it is unlikely in the immediate future to result in less thin-ideal images existing and/or minimising the negative impact that the thin-ideal can have for some women.

This chapter will discuss these challenges, which fit into two main categories. The first are associated with the content contained in Body Image Law. These are: (1) a comprehensive body of research that found that disclaimers on modified images are ineffective (this is part of the Israeli, French and Norwegian Body Image Laws and various bills and policy discussed in Chapter 5); (2) body mass index (BMI) is an inaccurate measure (the Israeli Body Image Law uses this measure to decide whether models can work, and the French Body Image Law takes it into consideration); and (3) Body Image Law does not cover non-commercial images (e.g. images of family, friends and acquaintances), so even in a jurisdiction with a Body Image Law that people abide by, people can still see thin-ideal images of their family, friends, acquaintances, etc.

The second category relates to challenges associated with implementing and enforcing Body Image Law and it includes: (1) challenges with implementing the Israeli Body Image Law and the difficulty to find evidence that the Body Image Laws in Israel, France and Norway are being enforced; (2) the significant number of harmful thin-ideal images online (making it difficult to enforce a Body Image Law); and (3) the fact that someone who lives in a country with a Body Image Law (even if people abide by it) might still see thin-ideal images from another country online (which could lessen the impact of the Body Image Law in their own country).

Addressing the problems with Body Image Law that this chapter discusses can be placed on a spectrum of easy to difficult. The author will discuss where on the spectrum each of the challenges to the Body Image Law lies.

Another challenge to Body Image Law, specifically in the United States, is the First Amendment, which protects freedom of speech and would make

DOI: 10.4324/9781003678793-6

it difficult to pass an effective Body Image Law there.[1] Discussing this constitutional issue is outside the purview of this book because it is outside the author's knowledge.

Challenges Associated with the Content of the Body Image Laws Themselves

Disclaimer Labels on Images Are Ineffective in the Body Image Law Context

A commonality of the French, Israeli and Norwegian Body Image Laws and the Body Image Bills that were proposed in Ontario (Canada),[2] Brazil,[3] the United Kingdom,[4] California (United States)[5] and Arizona (United States)[6] is that they all require images in which an advertiser digitally altered the body and/or shape of the model to add a disclaimer on the image that states that it was altered. Adding disclaimers to images of female models that were modified to make the model look thinner may seem like a good way to address the harm that seeing these images can cause because adding a disclaimer is likely cheap and easy.[7] Moreover, when people see images of women that were manipulated to make the model look thinner or to alter the model in some way, it is difficult for the average person to tell that the image was manipulated.[8]

1 *United States Constitution* amend I; Caitlin McBride et al, 'Digital Manipulation of Images of Models' Appearance in Advertising: Strategies for Action through Law and Corporate Social Responsibility Incentives to Protect Public Health' (2019) 45 *American Journal of Law & Medicine* 7, 14–15.

2 *Combatting Eating Disorders in Ontario Act, 2018,* Bill 29, 41st Leg, 3rd Sess, Ontario, 2018, s 2(2).

3 'PL 6.853/2010', *Câmara dos Deputados* [Chamber of Deputies] (5 March 2010) <https://www.camara.leg.br/proposicoesWeb/prop_mostrarintegra?codteor=740338>; *Projeto De Lei N.º 6.853-B, De 2010* [Bill No. 6,853-B, 2010] (Brazil), 24 February 2010.

4 UK Parliament, 'Digitally Altered Body Images Bill – Parliamentary Bills' (Web Page, 4 May 2021) <https://bills.parliament.uk/bills/2778>; *Digitally Altered Body Images Bill 2021* (U.K.).

5 Assembly Bill 2539, An Act to Add Section 1812.610 to the Civil Code, Relating to Employment of Models, 2015-16 Reg Sess, California, 2016 § 1707.2.

6 House Bill 2793, An Act Requiring Disclaimers on Digitally Altered Advertising Images, 50th Leg, 2nd Reg Sess (Ariz, 2012) § 1.

7 Belinda Bury, Marika Tiggemann and Amy Slater, 'The Effect of Digital Alteration Disclaimer Labels on Social Comparison and Body Image: Instructions and Individual Differences' (2015) 17 *Body Image* 136, 136.

8 Sophie J Nightingale, Kimberley A Wade and Derrick G Watson, 'Can People Identify Original and Manipulated Photos of Real-World Scenes?' (2017) 2(1) *Cognitive Research: Principles and Implications* 1, 16.

You might assume that a disclaimer that states that an image was modified could encourage the viewer to critically analyse the image that they see,[9] and/or the viewer will not compare themselves to the image and seeing the image will harm their body image less.[10]

Unfortunately, researchers found that this assumption is incorrect. People usually do not interpret disclaimer labels on images the way that those advocating for such labels want them to.[11] A substantial amount of peer-reviewed research found that disclaimers are ineffective.[12] One of the papers on this topic stated that the disclaimers are 'of no benefit to body image'.[13] It does not matter if a disclaimer on an image is larger or smaller, it is still likely to be ineffective.[14]

The politicians who pass Body Image Laws, or try to, refer to evidence concerning how seeing thin-ideal images can lead some people to develop eating disorders,[15] but the author could not find that they refer to the evidence that disclaimers on images are ineffective.

9 Bury, Tiggemann and Slater (n 7) 136.

10 Marika Tiggemann et al, 'Disclaimer Labels on Fashion Magazine Advertisements: Effects on Social Comparison and Body Dissatisfaction' (2013) 10 *Body Image* 45, 46.

11 Marika Tiggemann, Zoe Brown and Isabella Anderberg, 'Effect of Digital Alteration Information and Disclaimer Labels Attached to Fashion Magazine Advertisements on Women's Body Dissatisfaction' (2019) 30 *Body Image* 221, 226.

12 See, for example, Z Brown and M Tiggemann, 'A Picture Is Worth a Thousand Words: The Effect of Viewing Celebrity Instagram Images with Disclaimer and Body Positive Captions on Women's Body Image' (2020) (33) *Body Image* 190, 195; Francesca Giorgianni, Elisa Danthinne and Rachel F Rodgers, 'Consumer Warning versus Systemic Change: The Effects of Including Disclaimer Labels on Images That Have or Have Not Been Digitally Modified on Body Image' (2020) 34 *Body Image* 249, 255; Nehama Lewis, Ayellet Pelled and Nurit Tal-Or, 'The Effect of Exposure to Thin Models and Digital Modification Disclaimers on Women's Body Satisfaction' (2020) 55(2) *International Journal of Psychology* 245, 250; Julianne Livingston, Elise Holland and Jasmine Fardouly, 'Exposing Digital Posing: The Effect of Social Media Self-Disclaimer Captions on Women's Body Dissatisfaction, Mood, and Impressions of the User' (2020) 32 *Body Image* 150, 153; Marika Tiggemann et al, 'Disclaimer Labels on Fashion Magazine Advertisements: Effects on Social Comparison and Body Dissatisfaction' (2017) 25 *Eating Behaviors: An International Journal* 45, 51; Leila Selimbegović and Armand Chatard, 'Single Exposure to Disclaimers on Airbrushed Thin Ideal Images Increases Negative Thought Accessibility' (2015) 12 *Body Image* 1, 3–4.

13 Elisa S Danthinne, Francesca E Giorgianni and Rachel F Rodgers, 'Labels to Prevent the Detrimental Effects of Media on Body Image: A Systematic Review and Meta-Analysis' (2020) 53(5) *The International Journal of Eating Disorders* 647–661, 658.

14 Nehama Lewis, Ayellet Pelled and Nurit Tal-Or, 'The Effect of Exposure to Thin Models and Digital Modification Disclaimers on Women's Body Satisfaction' (2020) 55(2) *International Journal of Psychology* 245, 250.

15 For instance, the proposed Brazilian Body Image Bill. See, 'PL 6.853/2010', *Câmara dos Deputados* [Chamber of Deputies] (5 March 2010) <https://www.camara.leg.br/proposicoesWeb/prop_mostrarintegra?codteor=740338>; *Projeto De Lei N.º 6.853-B, De 2010* [Bill No. 6,853-B, 2010] (Brazil), 24 February 2010, art 1.

In addition, there is a danger that a law requiring a disclaimer on images of models that were digitally altered to make the model look thinner could have unintended consequences. A requirement that an advertiser add a disclaimer to any images that were modified may have the tragic effect that, to avoid the need to modify images (and require the disclaimer), advertisers will seek out unhealthily thin models. This could encourage models, or aspiring models, to undertake unhealthy practices to be ultra-thin to obtain such work. For example, they might have cosmetic surgery, exercise compulsively or eat insufficient amounts of food.[16] While the author could not find evidence that this is currently occurring through examining legal and public health databases in June 2025, that is not to say that it is not happening or would not happen, given the possible strong motivation involved.

Part of addressing the challenge that disclaimers on thin-ideal images are ineffective is, in some ways, easy from a legal perspective. The Israeli, French and Norwegian Governments can modify their Body Image Laws to remove the sections pertaining to this. However, the governments would need to add Body Image Law to their legislative agendas, which may be difficult due to competing priorities.

Problems with Using BMI

The Israeli Body Image Law states that models must have a minimum BMI to model and the French Body Image Law takes BMI into consideration, but there are challenges with using BMI as a measure to evaluate models' health. Belgian Adolphe Quetelet created the BMI in the 1830s; the formula involves dividing a person's weight in kilograms by their height in metres squared.[17] People use it to measure body fat.[18] Having a BMI under 18.5 is considered underweight and a 18.5–24.9 BMI is seen as normal.[19] A BMI of 25–29.9 is deemed overweight and a BMI over 30 is regarded as obese.[20] A healthy BMI can be different across ethnicities, races and ages.[21] One of the problems with using BMI is that it treats fat the same as muscle, bone and other tissues, so

16 Allyson Chiu, 'Why Experts Say Norway's Retouched Photo Law Won't Help Fight Body Image Issues', *The Washington Post* (online, 8 July 2021) <https://www.washingtonpost.com/lifestyle/wellness/photo-edit-social-media-norway/2021/07/08/f30d59ca-df2c-11eb-ae31-6b7c5c34f0d6_story.html>.

17 Stephen Humphreys, 'The Unethical Use of BMI in Contemporary General Practice' (2010) 60(578) *British Journal of General Practice* 696, 696.

18 Buss (n 21) 264.

19 Ibid.

20 Humphreys (n 17) 696.

21 Julia Buss, 'Limitations of Body Mass Index to Assess Body Fat' (2014) 62(6) *AAOHN Journal* 264, 264. Also see: Katherine L Record and Bryn S Austin, '"Paris Thin": A Call to Regulate Life-Threatening Starvation of Runway Models in the US Fashion Industry' (2016) 106(2) *American Journal of Public* 205, 205.

someone who has a lot of muscle could wrongly appear to have a high BMI.[22] Addressing this challenge with the Israeli and French Body Image Laws is arguably not difficult (assuming that it is politically palatable for those governments to modify their Body Image Laws): legislators can modify their Body Image Law so that a model's inability to work is based on a different indicator than BMI.

Seeing Non-Commercial Images

A further challenge with Body Image Law is that it regulates commercial images and does not regulate non-commercial images that viewers may see on social media: those of friends, acquaintances[23] and family members. It would be impossible to regulate non-commercial images.

Assuming that Body Image Law successfully significantly lowers the number of thin-ideal images, women may still see non-commercial thin-ideal images, perhaps of their family, friends and acquaintances. This book stated in its first chapter that the average weight of a model is far lower than the average woman's. So, it is possible that when women see the non-commercial images of their family, friends, acquaintances, etc. they will primarily see images of average weight women, as opposed to the thin-ideal (which would be better for their body image). That non-commercial images do not fall under Body Image Law is not easy to address, due to the ubiquitous nature of such images.

Problems Associated with Implementing and Enforcing the Laws

Challenges with Enforcing the Israeli Body Image Law and with Finding Evidence That the Israeli, French and Norwegian Laws Are Being Enforced

The proposed amendment to the original Israeli Body Image Law stated that there were no ways to 'enforce and supervise' the law.[24] The only current way to deal with breaches of this law is to start a class action lawsuit (which this book previously discussed), with all the difficulties and costs this could involve.

22 Humphreys (n 17) 264.

23 Michael Stuart, 'Failure to Influence: Legislation Requiring Social Media Influencers to Disclose their Retouched Images will not Address Youth Body Image Concerns' (2024) 31(2) *University of Miami International and Comparative Law Review* 463, 491.

24 הצעת חוק הגבלת משקל בענף הדוגמנות תיקון – הוראות שונות [Law for Restricting Weight in the Modelling Industry] (Amendment – Various Provisions), 2 September 2022, 5776-2016 (P/2825/20).

There is also evidence that the Israeli Body Image Law is having little legal impact. A report by the Knesset stated that their staff asked the Israeli Medical Association, four health funds and a modelling agency for information on how many medical certificates from models stating their BMI they had received since the law came into force, but were told that this information did not exist.[25] They also asked for information on implementing the requirement about the disclaimer when images were digitally altered.[26] They learned that only a brief study about this was undertaken, by students, and they could not find any disclaimers on digitally altered images.[27] They also asked the Israeli courts administration about whether there were any lawsuits pursuant to the Body Image Law and were told that the information could not be provided.[28] This information is from a report that was released in 2017;[29] more recent information about the current state of implementing the Israeli Body Image Law would be helpful.

There is a little cursory evidence that French advertisers are at least partially implementing the French Body Image Law: a researcher saw the French disclaimer being used in some French Metro stations.[30] Also, as stated in Chapter 5, researchers asked models who participated in Fashion Week in New York in 2018 about whether they planned to participate in Fashion Week in Paris, and if so, whether they obtained a health certificate for it and which health indicators their doctor assessed.[31] All 15 of the models who stated that they planned to participate in French Fashion Week in Paris obtained a health certificate for it.[32]

The author could not find any evidence of the Norwegian Body Image Law being implemented. However, it is the most recent Body Image Law passed, and evidence may be readily available over time. Further evidence on implementing the Body Image Law is critical to analyse how successful it is

25 Renana Gutreich, *Implementation and Enforcement of the Law for Restricting Weight in the Modeling Industry, 5772-2012* (The Knesset Research and Information Center, 7 June 2017) 5 <https://m.knesset.gov.il/EN/activity/mmm/me04076.pdf>.

26 Ibid.

27 Ibid.

28 Ibid 6.

29 Ibid.

30 Elisa S. Danthinne and Rachel F. Rodgers, '"Photographie Retouchée": Using Policy to Address Body Image' (2020) 20(1) *Harvard Undergraduate Health Policy Review* <https://www.huhpr.org/volume-20-issue-1-2/2020/9/15/photographic-reoutchee-using-policy-to-address-body-image>; 'How Have "Model Health" Laws Actually Impacted the Fashion Industry?', *The Fashion Law* (12 October 2020) <https://www.thefashionlaw.com/how-have-fashions-model-laws-impacted-the-fashion-industry/>.

31 Rachel F Rodgers et al, 'Disordered Eating Behaviors and Sexual Objectification during New York Fashion Week: Implementation of Industry Policies and Legislation' (2021) 54(3) *The International Journal of Eating Disorders* 433, 435.

32 Ibid.

and whether politicians should modify it or parts thereof or if politicians in other jurisdictions should implement similar laws or parts thereof. Of course, whether a Body Image Law is enforced (particularly in France and Norway) depends, among other things, on whether a government prioritises it, and priorities can change quickly and over time.

COVID-19 and its aftermath may have also changed public health priorities in the jurisdictions with a Body Image Law, so enforcing it may not have been as important during the pandemic and afterwards. Indeed, COVID-19 and its aftermath may be the reason why there have been few new Body Image Laws or bills introduced in the past five or so.

High Number of Images Online

Another challenge with Body Image Law is that there are a significant number of thin-ideal images that government officials would need to review to enforce it[33], and in Israel, many class action lawsuits would be necessary to address the thin-ideal images there. However, if even one class action lawsuit was successful in Israel, that might be a valuable deterrent to other advertisers to abide by the law, which might make additional class action lawsuits unnecessary.

The challenge of a significant number of thin-ideal images appearing online is not easy to address. Government officials could try reviewing a representative sample of images in their respective countries, perhaps using artificial intelligence, to lessen the amount of resources involved. Also, if government staff only review some images, and advertisers do not know which, this could potentially create a deterrent effect that results in advertisers applying the Body Image Law equally to all of their images. Given how many of such images exist, it would seem that government staff would only be able to review some images anyway.

Seeing Images from Other Jurisdictions

Another challenge with Body Image Law is the international nature of the internet. A person who uses social media and the internet in a country with a Body Image Law can still easily and quickly access material online that individuals in other countries without a Body Image Law post. Consequently, they can still potentially see countless thin-ideal images, thereby possibly lessening the impact of the original Body Image Law significantly.

33 Stuart (n 23) 493.

If, in an ideal world, all countries had an effective Body Image Law that they enforced, this would not be an issue. However, an ideal world is not one in which we live.

The Israeli Body Image Law states that an advertisement will not breach it if it does not appear to be intended for the Israeli people.[34] That is, if an Israeli advertiser creates an advertisement with the thin-ideal in it, for example, for the people of Canada, the image does not breach the Israeli Body Image Law. This statement does not solve the situation at hand, but it indicates that the Israeli Government appeared to think about some of the international complications arising from the law. Neither the text of the French nor the Norwegian Body Image Law appears to contemplate this conundrum.

A way to potentially circumvent this challenge, or to modify the legislation pertaining to online safety of a country with a Body Image Law, would be to include in a Body Image Law a statement that the country's internet must block content from overseas jurisdictions that breaches the Body Image Law. In the United States, the courts would be unlikely to uphold such a law because of section 230 of the Communications Decency Act:[35] American courts interpreted this federal legislation as barring plaintiffs from successfully suing social media companies for actions that its users took that breached many types of laws.[36] In contrast, in Australia, the High Court decided that plaintiffs can successfully sue social media companies when users breach law on their platforms.[37]

Such legislative action may be possible in other jurisdictions. For example, the Online Safety Act (2003) in the United Kingdom tries to make the internet safer.[38] The legislation's definition of 'Primary Priority Content' includes content that 'encourages, promotes or provides instructions for an eating disorder or behaviours associated with an eating disorder'.[39] Social media platforms must undertake various risk assessments, such as in relation to the risk that 'Primary Priority Content' poses to children.[40] Social media must also prevent children from seeing 'Primary Priority Content'[41] and explain how they will do so in their terms of service.[42] In the United Kingdom, theoretically, it would be possible for the Federal Government to modify the Online Safety

34 הדוגמנות בענף משקל הגבלת חוק הצעת [Law for Restricting Weight in the Modelling Industry], 27 March 2012, 5772-2012 s 4.

35 47 USC § 230 (1996).

36 See e.g., *Caraccioli v. Facebook, Inc.*, 700 F. App'x. 588 (9th Cir. 2017), *Cohen v. Facebook, Inc.*; 252 F. Supp. 3d 140 (E.D.N.Y. 2017); *Nunes v. Twitter, Inc.*, 194 F. Supp. 3d 959, 967 (N.D. Cal. 2016); *Carafano v. Metrosplash.com, Inc.*, 339 F.3d 1119, 1122, 1125 (9th Cir. 2003).

37 *Fairfax Media Publications Pty Ltd v. Voller* (2021) 273 CLR 346.

38 Online Safety Act 2003 (U.K.) s 1.

39 Ibid s 61(5).

40 Ibid s 11(6).

41 Ibid ss 12(3), 12(4).

42 Ibid s 12(9).

Act to broaden the definition of 'Primary Priority Content' to include content that breaches a Body Image Law, whether the material is posted domestically or overseas (if the Federal Government passed a Body Image Law).

In Australia, in 2024, there was a review of the Online Safety Act 2021 (Cth), legislation that tries to make the internet safer for Australians.[43] It recommended that the Australian Federal Government creates a digital duty of care for social media to 'take reasonable steps to prevent foreseeable harm',[44] which covers material that includes or promotes disordered eating.[45] In November 2024, the Australian Federal Minister for Communications, Michelle Rowland, announced that the Federal Government intended to pass legislation to establish a digital duty of care.[46] If it does so, it could include that social media has a duty to take reasonable steps to prevent foreseeable harm regarding material that breaches Body Image Law that is posted domestically or abroad (if the Australian Federal Government passes a Body Image Law).

This book occasionally considers tobacco control as an example of governments successfully addressing advertising/images negatively impacting health. It may provide some useful guidance for Body Image Law: it is well known that seeing advertising/images of tobacco can encourage people to smoke, particularly young people.[47] Many tobacco advertisements/images are online and people in one country can see advertisements/images online from another country, so it is an international problem.[48]

43 Ibid s 3.

44 Delia Rickard, *Report of the Statutory Review of the Online Safety Act 2021* (Commonwealth of Australia, October 2024) 7 <https://www.infrastructure.gov.au/department/media/publications/report-statutory-review-online-safety-act-2021>.

45 Ibid.

46 Michelle Rowland, Minister for Communications, 'New Duty of Care Obligations on Platforms Will Keep Australians Safer Online' (Media Release, 14 November 2024) <https://minister.infrastructure.gov.au/rowland/media-release/new-duty-care-obligations-platforms-will-keep-australians-safer-online, https://minister.infrastructure.gov.au/rowland/media-release/new-duty-care-obligations-platforms-will-keep-australians-safer-online>.

47 *Expert Group on Tobacco Advertising, Promotion and Sponsorship: Depiction of Tobacco in Entertainment Media Report by the Expert Group* (No FCTC/COP/8/7, Conference of the Parties to the W.H.O. Framework Convention on Tobacco Control, 27 June 2018) [11]–[12] <https://iris.who.int/bitstream/handle/10665/370643/fctc-cop8-7-en.pdf?sequence=1>; Adriana Pérez et al, 'The Longitudinal Impact of Seeing and Posting Tobacco-Related Social Media on Tobacco Use Behaviors Among Youth (Aged 12-17): Findings From the 2014-2016 Population Assessment of Tobacco and Health (PATH) Study' (2022) 15 *Tobacco Use Insights* 1, 6; Erin A Vogel et al, 'Young Adults' Exposure to and Engagement with Tobacco-Related Social Media Content and Subsequent Tobacco Use' (2024) 26(Supplement 1) *Nicotine & Tobacco Research* S1, S7.

48 *Expert Group on Tobacco Advertising, Promotion and Sponsorship: Depiction of Tobacco in Entertainment Media Report by the Expert Group* (No FCTC/COP/8/7, Conference of the Parties to the W.H.O. Framework Convention on Tobacco Control, 27 June 2018) [12] <https://iris.who.int/bitstream/handle/10665/370643/fctc-cop8-7-en.pdf?sequence=1>.

The World Health Organization Framework on Tobacco Control ('W.H.O. Tobacco Framework') is an evidence-based treaty on tobacco control[49] with 168 signatories.[50] Article 13 of the W.H.O. Tobacco Framework states each party to it will ban tobacco advertising and there will be 'a comprehensive ban on cross-border advertising'.[51] It further says that the parties will work together to create technology to eliminate cross-border advertising.[52] It also states that the parties will consider creating guidelines with details of how they will collaborate on their cross-border advertising and promotion ban.[53]

The parties to the W.H.O. Tobacco Framework created an Expert Group with representatives from different countries who collaborate with it to consider how tobacco appears in the media and give recommendations on cross-border tobacco advertising.[54] One of the Expert Group's recommendations is that they work together on the cross-border challenge of people in one jurisdiction being able to view tobacco promotion in another.[55] A document which elaborated on the guidelines to implement Article 13 of the W.H.O. Tobacco Framework states that responsibility to uphold it should be broad, and it should include everyone involved in the marketing chain, but primary responsibility lies with the advertising's creator.[56]

Politicians in countries with Body Image Law could follow tobacco's lead: they could form a similar expert group to work collaboratively together to help each other to prevent the public from seeing thin-ideal images across borders and share best practices regarding technology. They can also continue to look to the expert group associated with the W.H.O. Tobacco Framework to learn if they took any actions or created any documents that could be useful to consider to address cross-border issues associated with Body Image Law.

Since a lot of organisation and cooperation among people in different countries would be necessary to address cross-border advertising relating to Body Image Law, this is a challenging problem to address.

49 W.H.O. Framework Convention on Tobacco Control, 'W.H.O. Framework Convention on Tobacco Control' <https://iris.who.int/bitstream/handle/10665/42811/9241591013.pdf?sequence=1> v.

50 Ibid vi.

51 Ibid Article 13(2).

52 Ibid Article 13(6)

53 Ibid Article 13(8).

54 *Expert Group on Tobacco Advertising, Promotion and Sponsorship: Depiction of Tobacco in Entertainment Media Report by the Expert Group* (n 48) [5].

55 Ibid (n 48) [14a].

56 *Elaboration of Guidelines for Implementation of Article 13 of the Convention* (No FCTC/COP/3/9, Conference of the Parties to the W.H.O. Framework Convention on Tobacco Control, 2 September 2008) [53] <https://apps.who.int/gb/fctc/PDF/cop3/FCTC_COP3_9-en.pdf>.

Should Body Image Law Exist at All?

The research discussed in the book to date might make you wonder whether a Body Image Law should exist at all. Maybe the author should find research areas with greater potential to help the public and with more robust evidence to examine (and maybe she should have done so before writing several thousand words on this topic).

Moreover, perhaps efforts in the body image and eating disorders area might be better spent on providing eating disorder prevention programmes, which can help lessen eating disorder symptoms[57] and body dissatisfaction.[58] Also, maybe efforts should be spent on teaching media literacy, which can help to lower the feeling of needing to be thin,[59] or teaching social media literacy, which has been found to make people feel better about their body.[60] These initiatives, while extremely important and necessary, do not address one of the roots of the problem: the ubiquitous existence of thin-ideal images. Nor is it realistic for every single person to attend an eating disorder prevention programme or receive media literacy or social media literacy training. It is also unrealistic for the education/media literacy/social media literacy to impact all people who received them in the way that the people who delivered them intended.

Since Body Image Law has different components, the author will discuss whether there should be a Body Image Law by considering its two main components separately.

One part of Body Image Law involves adding disclaimers to images of models that were modified. Since, as described previously, these disclaimers are ineffective, the author suggests that no other governments pass similar laws or create comparable policy. It is unethical to require the disclaimer when it can worsen body image and to demand that the advertising industry fulfils this obligation or else face a legal penalty.

The other component of Body Image Law consists of obligations involving models' bodies: models must have a minimum BMI of 18.5[61] or have

57 Eric Stice et al, 'An Effectiveness Trial of a Dissonance-Based Eating Disorder Prevention Program for High-Risk Adolescent Girls' (2009) 77(5) *Journal of Consulting and Clinical Psychology* 825, 832–833 ('An Effectiveness Trial').

58 Eric Stice et al, 'Evaluation of a Novel Eating Disorder Prevention Program for Young Women with Type 1 Diabetes: A Preliminary Randomized Trial' (2023) 206 *Diabetes Research and Clinical Practice* 1, 5; Stice et al, 'An Effectiveness Trial' (n 57) 832–833.

59 Siân A McLean, Susan J Paxton and Eleanor H Wertheim, 'The Role of Media Literacy in Body Dissatisfaction and Disordered Eating: A Systematic Review' (2016) 19 *Body Image* 9, 20.

60 Siân A McLean et al, 'A Pilot Evaluation of a Social Media Literacy Intervention to Reduce Risk Factors for Eating Disorders' (2017) 50(7) *The International Journal of Eating Disorders* 847, 851.

61 תונמגודה ףנעב לקשמ תלבגה קוח תעצה [Law for Restricting Weight in the Modelling Industry], 27 March 2012, 5772-2012, ss 1, 2(a).

their health assessed overall, to ensure that it is compatible with modelling.[62] Researchers should consider investigating the impact of this specific limb of Body Image Law, which exists in Israel and France. If it positively affected body image, then governments should consider keeping this part of the Body Image Law, and politicians in other jurisdictions should think about passing similar laws. Nevertheless, the Israeli and French Governments should contemplate removing BMI from their Body Image Law and replacing it with another measurement.

This book previously described a research study involving the Israeli Body Image Law, which found that in the younger age group of Israeli study participants, 81 women aged 18–24, the law moderately changed their beliefs about the thin-ideal.[63] This evidence supports that Body Image Law demands, at the very least, more research.

Some people argue that health, and particularly mental health, is the responsibility of the individual, and not the community,[64] and the government does not have a responsibility to try to help improve it. Similar arguments can likely be made for other public health initiatives, such as smoking, and even wearing seat belts. It is clear that government intervention, by legislation and otherwise, was critical to achieve current low rates of smoking traditional cigarettes and saving countless lives. So, it is worth considering whether it can also be helpful, to some extent, in the Body Image Law context.

Body Image Law received considerable publicity. You might think that it would be worthwhile for politicians to pass a Body Image Law if only to gain publicity for poor body image, eating disorders and the connection between seeing thin-ideal images and poor body image and eating disorders, even if it is not actively enforced or even if it has no more than a slight or even an unascertainable effect on body image and eating disorders.

This raises the question of what is the point of passing a law if it is uncertain whether it will be effective. There are other ways to raise attention for an important issue than to pass a law. Given the limited resources most governments have, it can be argued that it is not a good use of time or public resources to pass a law just to raise awareness. Perhaps instead people with marketing experience and knowledge could be responsible for raising awareness, as opposed to politicians debating and passing legislation or creating policy: publicity and awareness should be an added benefit of legislation, not its main purpose.

62 *Code du travail* [Labour Code] (France) art L. 7123-2-1.

63 Michal Cohen and Yael Latzer, 'The Impact of Israel's "Models' Law" on Young Women' (2021) 13(4) *International Journal of Psychological Studies* 32, 43–44.

64 Susan J Paxton, 'Social Policy and Prevention' in Michael P Levine and Linda Smola (eds), *The Wiley Handbook of Eating Disorders* (John Wiley & Sons, Ltd, 2015) 663.

Also, it has been argued that Body Image Law discriminates against models who are naturally the thin-ideal and healthy: they could lose their jobs.[65] That would obviously be unfortunate but applying a utilitarian approach, the overall health of the public should take priority over a likely relatively small number of models losing their jobs.

The Israeli Freedom of Occupation Law states that every Israeli has the right to work in any occupation, profession or trade.[66] Israelis can breach this law no more than they need to, and only if the law in question reflects Israel's values and is for a proper purpose.[67] When the Israeli Body Image Law went before the Knesset before it was passed, the Knesset's Legal Committee stated that the law breached the Israeli Freedom of Occupation Law. Supporters of the law stated that the Israeli Body Image Law only breached the Freedom of Occupation Law for a few models, but not supporting it would hurt countless young women who internalised the thin-ideal.[68]

Job losses, unfortunately, can result from prioritising public health. For example, tobacco control policies caused job losses in the tobacco industry.[69] Politicians could also modify Body Image Law to address the problem of some models losing their jobs due to introducing a Body Image Law which forbids them from working because their body type is the thin-ideal. The government could give them some financial compensation or pay for retraining to an area other than modelling.

Thinking about this issue from another, broader, perspective, if Body Image Law helps lower the number of thin-ideal images in advertising, it could help send a message that the world (and in particular, the advertising and fashion industry and influencers) needs to stop creating harmful artificial ideals for women's bodies: while in ancient times this was foot binding or wearing corsets (which this book mentioned in its first chapter) and currently it is the thin-ideal, these pressures must stop.

65 'Skinny Models Banned', *Sydney Morning Herald* (online, 13 September 2006) <https://www.smh.com.au/lifestyle/fashion/skinny-models-banned-20060913-gdodrf.html>.

66 חוק-יסוד: חופש העיסוק [Basic Law: Freedom of Occupation (Israel)] 1994.

67 Ibid s 4.

68 Yael Latzer, Rachel Adatto and Dianne Neumark-Sztainer, 'Addressing Eating Disorders through Legislation: The Israeli "Models' Law" – Process, Enactment, and Dilemmas' (2022) 1 *Dialogues in Health* 1, 3.

69 'Employment Impact of Tobacco Control' in *The Economics of Tobacco and Tobacco Control* (U.S. Department of Health and Human Services, National Institutes of Health, National Cancer Institute; and Geneva, CH: World Health Organization, 2016) 543 <https://cancercontrol.cancer.gov/sites/default/files/2020-06/m21_15.pdf>.

Conclusion

This chapter outlined the challenges with Body Image Law in two main categories: those pertaining to the laws themselves and others that relate to enforcing them. Some of these challenges appear easy to address: parts of disclaimers being ineffective and BMI not being a valid measure to consider whether models can work. Some are more complicated: the ubiquitous nature of non-commercial thin-ideal images, thin-ideal images online generally and cross-border advertising.

This chapter also discussed whether Body Image Law should exist at all. Since Body Image Law has the potential to help address the crux of the harm that seeing thin-ideal images can cause, the proliferating number of thin-ideal images, the area is worth researching and considering further.

7 Pro-Anorexia Websites/Social Media and the Law

Introduction

This book, to date, has discussed harmful images that the advertising industry created. It will now discuss a different type of damaging images and posts: Pro-Ana and Pro-Mia content, which promote eating disorders as a lifestyle choice, as opposed to an illness.[1] This content is 'a long-standing societal concern'[2] and has a different creator from thin-ideal images: people who have eating disorders.[3]

People use the terms 'Pro-Ana' and 'Pro-Mia' interchangeably, and the literature in the area focuses on the impact of Pro-Anorexia Nervosa content.[4] This book uses the words 'Pro-Ana' to refer to both Pro-Anorexia Nervosa and Pro-Bulimia material. While some of the literature on this topic discusses Pro-Ana content on websites, as opposed to on social media, the facts and ideas that this chapter will consider, generally, apply to both.

Pro-Ana content can include advice on purging and starving,[5] photos of thin celebrities and models and of the people who create the content, plus poetry and song lyrics promoting eating disorders.[6] They may also contain quotes to inspire people to diet and links to other Pro-Ana content,[7] 'thin-

1 Anna M Bardone-Cone and Kamila M Cass, 'What Does Viewing a Pro-Anorexia Website Do? An Experimental Examination of Website Exposure and Moderating Effects' (2007) 40(6) *The International Journal of Eating Disorders* 537, 538; Mario Christodoulou, 'Pro-Anorexia Websites Pose Public Health Challenge' (2012) 379(9811) *The Lancet (British edition)* 110, 110.

2 Ysabel Gerrard, 'Beyond the Hashtag: Circumventing Content Moderation on Social Media' (2018) 20(12) *New Media & Society* 4492, 4493.

3 Antonio A. Casilli, Fred Pailler and Paola Tubaro, 'Online Networks of Eating-Disorder Websites: Why Censoring Pro-Ana Might Be a Bad Idea' (2013) 133(2) *Perspectives in Public Health* 94, 94.

4 Blair J Davis, 'The Experience of Bulimic College Students Who Use "Pro-Ana/Pro-Mia" Web Sites: A Two-Phase Mixed-Method Study' (ProQuest Dissertations & Theses, 2010) 3.

5 Casilli, Pailler, and Tubaro (n 3) 94; Daphna Yeshua-Katz, 'Online Stigma Resistance in the Pro-Ana Community' (2015) 25(10) *Qualitative Health Research* 1347, 1348.

6 Yeshua-Katz (n 5) 1348.

7 Bardone-Cone and Cass (n 1) 538.

DOI: 10.4324/9781003678793-7

spiration' material (images and messages that promote being thin) and 'bonespiration' content (images and messages that promote bones showing, e.g. ribs and the spine).[8]

Most of the people who visit Pro-Ana websites have eating disorders themselves; however, some are 'wannarexics': they want to have an eating disorder and believe that they can treat an eating disorder as a 'fad'.[9] The people responsible for Pro-Ana content try to keep 'wannarexics' from engaging with Pro-Ana content.[10]

Pro-Ana content is controversial.[11] Pro-Ana websites can encourage vulnerable people to develop an eating disorder, and viewing the content can make it harder for people with eating disorders to recover.[12] Even though Pro-Ana content online can harm, people with eating disorders may find that they receive support from others who create and engage with this content, which can be particularly helpful because they can remain anonymous.[13]

Some online Pro-Ana pages have warnings informing the viewer that their content may negatively impact vulnerable people.[14] A content warning with factual information about Anorexia Nervosa appeared to people who visited Pro-Ana websites prior to viewing the websites for a year.[15] About one-third of website visitors did not continue to view the websites after they saw the warning,[16] demonstrating the warning's value.

8 Evidence to House of Commons, Women and Equalities Committee (Parliament of the United Kingdom, Centre for Appearance Research) <https://committees.parliament.uk/writtenevidence/7943/pdf/>.

9 N Boero and CJ Pascoe, 'Pro-Anorexia Communities and Online Interaction: Bridging the "Pro-Ana" Body Online' (2012) 18(2) *Body & Society* 27, 39.

10 Ibid 29.

11 Suku Sukunesan, Minh Huynh and Gemma Sharp, 'Examining the Pro-Eating Disorders Community on Twitter Via the Hashtag #proana: Statistical Modeling Approach' (2021) 8(7) *JMIR Mental Health* 1, 2; Anna M Bardone-Cone and Kamila M Cass, 'What Does Viewing a Pro-Anorexia Website Do? An Experimental Examination of Website Exposure and Moderating Effects' (2007) 40(6) *The International Journal of Eating Disorders* 537, 538.

12 Mario Christodoulou, 'Pro-Anorexia Websites Pose Public Health Challenge' (2012) 379(9811) *The Lancet* (British edition) 110, 110.

13 JL Harshbarger et al, 'Pro-Anorexia Websites: What a Clinician Should Know' (2009) 42 *International Journal of Eating Disorders*, 367, 367.

14 Dawn B Branley and Judith Covey, 'Pro-Ana versus Pro-Recovery: A Content Analytic Comparison of Social Media Users' Communication about Eating Disorders on Twitter and Tumbler' (2017) 8 *Frontiers in Psychology* 1, 5; Anna M Bardone-Cone and Kamila M Cass, 'What Does Viewing a Pro-Anorexia Website Do? An Experimental Examination of Website Exposure and Moderating Effects' (2007) 40(6) *The International Journal of Eating Disorders* 537, 538.

15 Carolien Martijn et al, 'Don't Get the Message: The Effect of a Warning Text before Visiting a Proanorexia Website' (2009) 42(2) *The International Journal of Eating Disorders* 139, 140, 141.

16 Ibid 143.

Law and Policy Regarding Pro-Anorexia Websites and Content

In 2012, online articles criticised social media employees for not stopping Pro-Ana content from appearing on their platforms. A few months later, the staff of Instagram, Pinterest and Tumblr announced that they would lower the amount of eating disorder content on their platforms.[17] They said that when users of their platforms searched for certain Pro-Ana hashtags, like #proana, they would send them a public service announcement.[18] Tumblr would send the following message when people looked for this kind of content:[19]

> [e]ating disorders are not lifestyle choices, they are mental disorders that when left untreated, can cause serious health problems, and at their most severe can even be life-threatening. For treatment referrals, information and support, please contact the National Eating Disorders Association's Helpline at 1-800-931-2237… www.nationaleatingdisorders.org.[20]

Tumblr's staff also worked with the National Eating Disorder Association ('N.E.D.A.'): the organisation would receive free or paid advertising every time anyone entered a word like 'pro-ana', 'anorexia' or 'thinspiration'.[21] Researchers questioned the relationship between Tumblr and N.E.D.A. because '[e]ven though the organisations featured in the PSAs may be non-profit, they benefit from the direct advertising because it leads to additional "business" which helps to legitimise the need for outside funding and donations'.[22] Nevertheless, the referrals to N.E.D.A. may genuinely help some of the people who see them, who may not otherwise know, or be in the state of mind, to search for an organisation that can help them. The author searched psychology and public health databases in March 2025 and was unable to find research about how effective the public service announcements are: meaning, whether they actually prevent people from searching for Pro-Ana content, and whether the recipients of the public service announcements actually try to contact any eating disorder not-for-profit organisations mentioned.

17 Gerrard (n 2) 4493.
18 Ibid.
19 Nicole Danielle Schott and Dera Langan, 'Pro-Anorexia/Bulimia Censorship and Public Service Announcements: The Price of Controlling Women' (2015) 37(8) *Media, Culture & Society* 1158, 1160.
20 Ibid 1161.
21 Ibid 1171.
22 Ibid.

Even though, in 2012, the staff of some social media platforms stated that they banned Pro-Ana content,[23] they have been unable to prevent it entirely from being on their platforms.[24]

In terms of Meta, in September 2021, Meta executive Antigone Davis testified before the U.S. Congress and stated that Meta 'do[es] not direct people towards content that promotes eating disorders. That actually violates our policies, and we remove that content when we become aware of it. We actually use AI to find content like that and remove it'.[25] Davis added that Meta works with experts on how to deal with eating disorder content.[26]

Meta staff stated that they would automatically restrict the Instagram and Facebook accounts of teenagers from harmful content, including eating disorder posts, and the changes were supposed to commence in January 2024. They would determine whether someone is a teenager from the birthdate that they entered when they joined the social media.[27] Teenagers are not supposed to be able to see or search for pro-eating disorder content, even if a friend or someone they follow shares it. When teenagers search for terms related to eating disorders, self-harm and suicide, Instagram and Facebook hide the results and send them information to get help.[28]

While it is helpful that Meta staff stated that they would automatically restrict the accounts of teenagers from harmful eating disorder content, they should also automatically restrict the accounts of adults from viewing this content. One reason for this is that a substantial number of young people lie about their age on social media,[29] so it is possible that teenagers who lied about their age and stated that they are adults see this material. The author searched psychology databases and the internet generally in March 2025 and could not find evidence that Pinterest and Tumblr limited their restrictions on Pro-Ana content to teenagers.

Meta's website stated that people infrequently view its content that contains suicide, self-injury and eating disorders and its staff remove most of this material. It further stated that in the fourth quarter of 2024, no more than five

23 Maia Szalavitz, 'Can Pro-Anorexia Websites Help Heal Some Eating Disorders?', *CNN* (online, 28 August 2012) <https://edition.cnn.com/2012/08/28/health/time-anorexia-websites/index.html>.

24 Casilli, Ailler and Tubaro (n 3) 94.

25 *Arizona & Ors v. Meta Platforms, Inc.*, 4:23-cv-05448 (N.D. Cal. Oct. 24, 2023), [334].

26 Ibid [336].

27 Julie Jargon, 'Instagram and Facebook Will Stop Treating Teens Like Adults; Efforts to Curb Harmful Material and Reduce Unwanted Interactions with Teen Social-Media Accounts Come as States Sue Parent Company Meta', *Wall Street Journal* (online, 9 January 2024) <https://www.wsj.com/tech/personal-tech/instagram-facebook-teen-content-restriction-meta-58e31d39>.

28 Ibid.

29 'A Third of Children Have Adult Social Media Accounts–Ofcom', *BBC* (online, 11 October 2022) <https://www.bbc.com/news/technology-63204605>.

out of every 10,000 views on their platforms had this kind of content.[30] While these statistics make it appear that Meta is successfully limiting the amount of Pro-Ana content on its platform, it does not state how much of this type of content, in total, is on its platform, nor does it state how many teenagers specifically see it. Both of these pieces of information would be helpful to evaluate how successful Meta's content restriction is.

Annexure C of this book contains the relevant parts of the current community standards for some social media (Meta, Snapchat, TikTok, X and YouTube) about Pro-Ana and body image-related content. Social media community standards apply to all social media users (including any content that artificial intelligence generates) and state what social media users are allowed to and not allowed to post.[31]

The parts of the current community standards that relate to Pro-Ana material and body image in Annexure C of this book all prohibit Pro-Ana content. Moreover, the content from Meta, Snapchat, TikTok and YouTube all refer users who post Pro-Ana content to resources (such as eating disorder not-for-profit organisations) that could help them. Interestingly, TikTok's community standard also gives examples of the kinds of eating disorder-related content that is and is not permitted. For example, promoting restrictive dieting is not allowed, but promoting eating competitions is.

Unfortunately, the majority of the community guidelines discussed do not consider that social media can be a safe space for some people with eating disorders to meet and support each other anonymously, in a way that does not promote eating disorders. It would be useful if they did, and explained the difference between people who have eating disorders using social media for support versus posting harmful Pro-Ana content. YouTube's community standard is the only one of those discussed that appears to come close. It states:

> YouTube users should not be afraid to speak openly about the topics of mental health, suicide, self-harm, and eating disorders in a supportive and non-harmful way. However, there are times when content is created that is sensitive and may pose a risk for some users. When you create content that contains suicide, self-harm, or eating disorder related topics, take into

30 Meta Inc., 'Community Standards Enforcement Report: Suicide, Self-Injury and Eating Disorders' <https://transparency.meta.com/reports/community-standards-enforcement/suicide-and-self-injury/instagram/>.

31 Meta Inc, 'Community Standards' <https://transparency.meta.com/en-gb/policies/community-standards>; TikTok, 'Community Standards' <https://www.tiktok.com/community-guidelines/en>.

account the possible negative impact of your content on other users, especially minors and users who may be sensitive to this content.[32]

Community standards are not law. So, if material on social media platforms breaches such standards (even if abundantly so), no legal consequences arise from this. However, from a public relations standpoint, they might be expected to do so, to avoid possible public backlash.

Reverting back to tobacco again, a beacon of light and hope regarding positive public health accomplishments, researchers (including the author) found that on TikTok, social media community standards relating to limiting content that promotes vaping were repeatedly and significantly breached.[33] This indicates, among other things, that we should consider whether the same is happening in relation to Pro-Ana content.

An investigation by *Wall Street Journal* journalists in 2001 involved their creating a dozen TikTok accounts that incorrectly stated that they belonged to 13-year-olds. They found that TikTok's algorithm sent them tens of thousands of weight-loss videos within a few weeks of creating the accounts. Some of the videos involved recommending consuming under 300 calories daily or only consuming water for entire days. Another suggested taking a laxative after eating. Others held a competition encouraging followers to lose as much weight as possible before the December break. After the journalists contacted TikTok and requested a response, TikTok representatives stated that they would modify their algorithm recommendation so that it would not show users too much of the same material and that it was testing ways to avoid showing its users too much content about certain topics, such as extreme dieting. They added that TikTok tries to remove content that breaches its community standards.[34]

Recommender systems prioritise content to people who use the internet.[35] Reset Australia, an organisation that focuses on research and policy, created fake social media accounts that looked like 16-year-olds made them.[36] They found that recommender systems promoted pro-eating disorder content to the

32 YouTube, 'Suicide, Self-Harm, and Eating Disorders Policy' (2025) <https://support.google.com/youtube/answer/2802245?hl=en>.

33 Jonine Jancey et al, 'Promotion of E-Cigarettes on TikTok and Regulatory Considerations' (2023) 20(10) *International Journal of Environmental Research and Public Health* 1, 7–8.

34 Tawnell D Hobbs, Rob Barry, and Yoree Koh, '"The Corpse Bride Diet": How TikTok Inundates Teens with Eating-Disorder Videos', *Wall Street Journal* (online, 17 December 2021) <https://www.wsj.com/articles/how-tiktok-inundates-teens-with-eating-disorder-videos-11639754848>.

35 eSafety Commissioner, 'Recommender Systems and Algorithms – Position Statement' (12 August 2022) <https://www.esafety.gov.au/industry/tech-trends-and-challenges/recommender-systems-and-algorithms>.

36 Reset.Tech Australia, *Not Just Algorithms: Assuring User Safety Online with Systemic Regulatory Frameworks* (Policy Report, March 2024) 3 <https://au.reset.tech/uploads/Not-Just-Algorithms-web-230323-V1.0.pdf>.

fake accounts;[37] none of the content that TikTok recommended was pro-eating disorder content, 23% of the content that Instagram recommended was pro-eating disorder content and 67% of the content that X recommended was pro-eating disorder content.[38] The study also found that there were challenges with moderating content: pro-eating disorder content was present on the social media, even though it violated the social media's own guidelines. TikTok staff removed 15.5% of the 110 posts that were reported to contain pro-eating disorder content, Instagram staff removed 6.3% of the 175 reported posts and X staff removed 6.0% of the 100 reported posts.[39] The report found that even though social media platforms may have comprehensive policies which state that they may remove pro-eating disorder content, the staff of the social media do not sufficiently enforce them, so some of the content remains.[40]

Both seeing thin-ideal images and Pro-Ana content can harm viewers and is related to body image and eating disorders, but there is another key reason why the author included a discussion of Pro-Ana material in this book. In 2015, the French Government, as part of its Body Image Law, proposed legislation which stated, '[c]ausing a person to seek excessive leanness by encouraging prolonged food restrictions which result in exposing the person to life-threatening danger or in directly compromising their health, is punishable by one year in prison and a fine of €10,000'.[41] This law, if passed, would have meant that people who create Pro-Ana content could receive a criminal conviction, a sentence of one year imprisonment and a fine of €10,000. Maud Olivier and Catherine Coutelle, who tabled the law, said that Pro-Ana content can 'cause people to become trapped in a "vicious circle of anorexia" that authorities are unable to tackle'.[42] The French National Assembly (Lower House of Parliament) passed the Bill, but the Senate (Upper House) did not.[43] The law may not have passed because of who creates Pro-Ana content.[44] They typically have eating disorders themselves,[45] so punishing them might make

37 Ibid.

38 Ibid.

39 Ibid.

40 Ibid.

41 *Loi n° 2016-41 du 26 janvier 2016 de modernisation de notre système de santé* [Law No 2016-41 of 26 January 2016 on the Modernisation of Our Health System] (France).

42 Heather Saul, 'People Running Pro-Anorexia and "thinspiration" Websites to Face Prison in France', *The Independent* (online, 9 April 2015) <https://www.independent.co.uk/life-style/health-and-families/health-news/people-running-thinspiration-or-proanorexia-websites-in-france-will-now-face-a-prison-sentence-and-maximum-ps7-000-fine-10153909.html>.

43 David I Benbow, '"Don't Panic, Don't Panic": An Analysis of a Purported Pro-Eating Disorder Website/Online Content Moral Panic and Legal and Policy Responses' [2024] *Information & Communications Technology Law* 1, 15.

44 Connor Bildfell, 'Legislating Away Illness: Examining Efforts to Curb the Development of Eating Disorders through Law' (2018) 26 *Dalhousie Journal of Legal Studies* 37, 52.

45 Casilli, Pailler and Tubaro (n 3) 94.

it harder for them to seek treatment.[46] Further, it could be harmful for people with a mental illness to have a criminal record and deal with the criminal justice system: this might negatively impact their health and ability to get a job in the future or keep their current one. Also, censoring Pro-Ana comments can make the people who use these websites think that even more people are against them.[47]

A better way to address this issue, and limit Pro-Ana content online while not punishing the people who create it, is similar to legislation that this book suggested in Chapter 5 which relates to dealing with thin-ideal images: pass legislation that fines social media a significant amount of money (an appropriate percentage of their revenue) when they do not have a reasonable plan to prevent Pro-Ana content from appearing on their platforms which they must implement, and also punish them if they do not act sufficiently quickly to remove the material if it appears on their platforms.

Chapter 5 of this book included a discussion of the Online Safety Act 2021 (Cth), legislation that tries to make the internet safer for Australians.[48] A review of this legislation suggested that the Australian Federal Government creates a digital duty of care for the staff of social media to 'take reasonable steps to prevent foreseeable harm',[49] which would contain material that includes or promotes disordered eating.[50] This would mean that staff of social media would need to try to restrict Pro-Ana content from appearing on their platforms. It appears from the discussion earlier in this chapter that this is already happening, without legislative intervention. Legislative intervention could put added pressure on social media to use their very best endeavours to address this issue.

Overall, it is more practical and just to hold social media accountable for Pro-Ana material appearing on social media platforms, rather than punish people who have eating disorders who typically create the content. Legislation that addresses Pro-Ana content can also stipulate that part or all of the money from the fines for breaching a law involving Pro-Ana content must go towards paying for eating disorder treatment and research (similar to the proposed

46 Marilyn Bromberg and Tomas Fitzgerald, 'Let's Starve Down to the Bone: Pro-Anorexia Websites and the Law' (2017) 25 *Journal of Law and Medicine* 124, 134.

47 Nicole Danielle Schott and Debra Langan, 'Pro-Anorexia/Bulimia Censorship and Public Service Announcements: The Price of Controlling Women' (2015) 37(8) *Media, Culture & Society* 1158, 1168.

48 Online Safety Act 2021 (Cth) s 3.

49 Delia Rickard, *Report of the Statutory Review of the Online Safety Act 2021* (Commonwealth of Australia, October 2024) 7 <https://www.infrastructure.gov.au/department/media/publications/report-statutory-review-online-safety-act-2021>.

50 Ibid 21.

amendment to the Israeli Body Image Law, in which money from fines for breaching the law would go to a fund to prevent and treat eating disorders).[51]

In 2023, the Texas Government passed the Social Media and Parental Oversight of Children's Exposure (Scope) Act,[52] which requires social media to develop and implement strategies to prevent young people under 18 from seeing content that 'promotes, glorifies, or facilitates' various harmful behaviours, including eating disorders,[53] and to use filtering technology and other methods to block this material.[54] Humans must monitor the filtering technology to ensure that it is effective.[55] It also requires social media to create and maintain a database of keywords that people use to try to evade the filtering technology and keep their harmful content online: it could include misspellings or certain hashtags.[56] If a social media platform breaches this law, then a child or their guardian who is affected can sue for a declaratory judgment or an injunction, but they cannot commence a class action.[57] The part of the law that requires social media to block harmful Pro-Ana content is a good idea because it theoretically should result in young people seeing less Pro-Ana content. Requiring a child or their guardian to commence such a lawsuit to enforce it is problematic, because they may not have sufficient resources to easily do so. Further, the remedies that the law offers to litigants are also disappointing: they are narrow and do not include being able to order social media to pay significant financial penalties, which could have a greater deterrent effect. It is also disappointing that the legislation prevents class action lawsuits, which could make it easier for people to sue the social media because of lower individual cost and increased efficiency.

Litigation commenced against this law: the judgment of one such lawsuit, against the Texas Attorney General in the United States District Court,[58] stated, among other things, that the law's restrictions on speech 'are unconstitutionally vague' and the part of the law that involved monitoring and filtering could not be enforced.[59] The case was appealed in the United States Supreme Court: their Honors decided that this case should be sent back to the lower court to make further decisions.[60] Their Honors also stated that the District

51 תונוש תוארוה – ןוקית תונמגודה ףנעב לקשמ תלבגה קוח תעצה [Law for Restricting Weight in the Modelling Industry] [(Amendment – Various Provisions)], 2 September 2022, 5776-2016 (P/2825/20).

52 Social Media and Parental Oversight of Children's Exposure (SCOPE) Act, Tex Gen Assem, HB 18, 88th Leg, Reg Sess (2023).

53 Ibid §§ 509.011, 509.503.

54 Ibid §509.053(b)(1)(B).

55 Ibid §509.053(b)(1)(E).

56 Ibid §509.053(b)(1)(D).

57 Ibid §509.152(b).

58 *NetChoice LLC v. Paxton*, 49 F4th 439 (5thCir, 2022).

59 Ibid 37–38.

60 *NetChoice LLC v. Paxton* (Supreme Court of the United States, No 22-555, 1 July 2024).

Court judgment did not include a proper analysis of how the law challenged the First Amendment.[61]

In another lawsuit concerning the SCOPE Act, adults who post social media content to minors, young people and representatives of Students Engaged in Advancing Texas, a coalition of students in middle school up to and including college, sued the Texas Attorney General regarding various issues arising from the SCOPE Act.[62] One of these issues involved an allegation that the legislation's monitoring and filtering requirements were void because they were vague.[63] Judge Pitman agreed that the filtering and monitoring requirements were vague and stated, among other things, that the Texas Attorney General could not enforce them.[64]

Also, in February 2025, Senator Renee Burgess introduced a bill in the New Jersey Legislature that involves holding social media responsible for Pro-Ana material on its platforms: it prohibits social media platforms from using 'a design, algorithm, practice, affordance, or feature' that it knows or should have known could cause people under age 18 to develop an eating disorder.[65] A social media platform does not breach this law if it can demonstrate that it regularly audits its algorithms, designs, etc. that could cause or contribute to children developing eating disorders on its platforms and it acts to correct breaches.[66] Social media platforms that breach this law could face a maximum civil penalty of $250,000 (U.S.).[67] At the time of writing, this bill is currently before the New Jersey Senate Health, Human Services and Senior Citizens Committee.[68]

The legislation does not explain what it means by encouraging people under age 18 to develop an eating disorder: what kind of material would be included. The author would hope that online groups that support young people who have eating disorders would not be included.

Conclusion

Pro-Ana content, which encourages people to develop and maintain an eating disorder, is shocking and harmful. The French Government introduced a bill

61 Ibid.

62 *Students Engaged in Advancing Texas v. Paxton*, No 1:24-CV-945-RP (WD, Tex, filed 7 February 2025) [2].

63 Ibid [44]–[45].

64 Ibid [44]–[54].

65 New Jersey Senate Bill S4153, 221st Legislature, Regular Session (introduced 25 February 2025). § 2(a).

66 Ibid § 2(b).

67 Ibid § 2(d).

68 Legiscan, 'NJ State Legislature Page for S4153' (Web Page) <https://legiscan.com/NJ/bill/S4153/2024>.

to punish the people who create it, but it did not become law. If it had, and it was enforced, it could have hurt the people who create the content, who typically have eating disorders. A more appropriate legal way to address this delicate and challenging issue appears to create or amend legislation to compel social media companies to use reasonable efforts to prevent this material from appearing on their platforms, remove it when it appears despite their best efforts and face significant financial penalties when they do not abide by the legislation.

8 What Might Work to Help Improve Body Image and Ways to Lower the Number of Unhelpful Images of the Thin-Ideal, Based on Evidence

Introduction

This chapter examines research regarding what actions, particularly those concerning thin-ideal images, could potentially help body image and, consequently, potentially form the basis of an effective Body Image Law.

Importantly, politicians should use evidence when they create a Body Image Law:[1] that is the crux of this chapter, and a foundational part of this book. This chapter provides such evidence. This is as opposed to using populist views to create Body Image Law because they may appeal to voters concerned about widespread poor body image and eating disorders, or any number of reasons for creating Body Image Law that are not based on evidence.

It is insufficient if politicians legislate in this area simply because people passionate about eating disorders advocate for it, or a politician has a personal experience with eating disorders, or a high-profile person dies from an eating disorder.[2]

When considering the content of a Body Image Law, politicians should consult with people who have lived experience of eating disorders[3] and work with researchers, clinicians, scientists, staff of social media platforms[4] and people in the fashion, beauty,[5] modelling and advertising industries as well as eating disorder advocates and staff from eating disorder not-for-profit organisations.

1 Evidence to House of Commons, Women and Equalities Committee (Parliament of the United Kingdom, Centre for Appearance Research) <https://committees.parliament.uk/writtenevidence/7943/pdf/>.

2 Susan J Paxton, 'Social Policy and Prevention' in Michael P Levine and Linda Smola (eds), *The Wiley Handbook of Eating Disorders* (John Wiley & Sons, Ltd, 2015) 663.

3 See, for example, Rachel Baffsky, 'Eating Disorders in Australia: A Commentary on the Need to Address Stigma' (2020) 8(1) *Journal of Eating Disorders* 1, 3.

4 Evidence to House of Commons (Ibid 1) 19.

5 Catarina de Freitas, Helen Jordan and Elizabeth K Hughes, 'Body Image Diversity in the Media: A Content Analysis of Women's Fashion Magazines' (2018) 29(3) *Health Promotion Journal of Australia* 251, 255.

DOI: 10.4324/9781003678793-8

These stakeholders' aims can vary considerably. While eating disorder advocates and staff from eating disorder not-for-profit organisations likely seek to legislate actions that they believe, and evidence substantiates, are best placed to help to improve body image, it is unrealistic to expect the interest of modelling and advertising industries simply to be ignored. Whilst profit and revenue would be very important to people in these industries, some do put public health over their bottom line, which this book outlined in Chapter 5. Balancing these aims is a challenge. Whenever possible, the wishes of fashion and advertising industries should be taken into account to try to lessen possible negative financial repercussions to them and create legislation that the industries are more likely to abide by.

When a government passes a Body Image Law, or any law, that does not automatically mean that people will abide by it. We know, as a general concept, some people break the law. There are many reasons why people may not abide by a law; for example, they may not know about it, they may not believe that they will be punished if they breach it or they may not agree with it. The last reason is why it is especially important for politicians to consult a broad range of stakeholders prior to creating a Body Image Law; the greater a consensus that can be reached, the greater the likely compliance with it.

The research regarding potentially effective measures to try to improve body image, which could possibly form the basis of a Body Image Law, falls under two main areas: (1) research that applies to thin-ideal images: using diverse models, showing unedited images next to edited images, displaying body positive content, not digitally altering images; and (2) research about measures external to thin-ideal images: rewarding businesses that use models who appear to have healthy bodies and tax-related actions. This chapter will briefly explain each of these measures and which may be most feasible overall.

This chapter will also explain the need to change the opinions of people in the beauty, advertising and fashion industries about initiatives that are positive for body image to try to encourage more people who work in these industries to work on body positive measures.

Research That Applies to the Images

Using Diverse Models

Many people in the advertising industry believe that using models who have larger bodies does not sell products, whereas using thin-ideal models does.[6]

6 Emma Halliwell and Helga Dittmar, 'Does Size Matter? The Impact of Model's Body Size on Women's Body-Focused Anxiety and Advertising Effectiveness' (2004) 23(1) *Journal of Social and Clinical Psychology* 104, 105.

Since advertisers believe that using thin-ideal models can increase their sales, it is unlikely that they would voluntarily decide to stop using them,[7] or they may choose not to abide by a Body Image Law that forbids them from doing so.

There is a compelling body of research that contradicts the advertising industry view. For example, a systemic review of 86 different studies that summarised the empirical findings on the effect of viewing models who were not the thin-ideal found that most studies discovered that viewing these types of models had positive or no effects on body image and advertising outcomes.[8]

Also, a study of 202 women in the United Kingdom, with an average age of 30.8, found that viewing thin-ideal models increased anxiety about their body, but seeing average-sized models did not, among women who are high internalisers.[9] Weight-related anxiety is significant because it can result in possible 'unhealthy weight loss behavio[u]rs'.[10] The study also found that how attractive a model is impacted the advertising's effectiveness, but the model's size did not.[11] This study is important because it demonstrates that advertisers can use average weight models (which is better for the health of viewers of their advertisements to see) and they will likely sell a similar number of products than if they used thin-ideal models.[12] Similarly, an Australian study with 291 women and men enrolled at a large Australian university[13] found that using average-sized models in advertisements can be good for the body image of the young women who see them while not negatively impacting the advertising's effectiveness.[14]

A U.K. Body Image inquiry report stated that the U.K. Government needs to urgently prioritise displaying more advertising of models with diverse bodies, ethnicities, sexualities and genders. It further stated that the government should work with companies and the Advertising Standards Authority to make this happen.[15] In Australia, Zoe Daniel M.P. and the Butterfly Foundation organised a roundtable with body image experts, including the author, who met between September 2023 and May 2024 to make recommendations to

7 Britney Clasper, 'Conceptualising a preventative approach to eating disorders in New Zealand' [2023] *New Zealand Law Students' Law Journal* 105, 156.

8 Orpha de Lenne et al, 'Experimental Research on Non-Idealized Models: A Systematic Literature Review' (2022) 47 *Body Image* 1, 29–32.

9 Halliwell and Dittmar (n 6) 119.

10 Ibid 119.

11 Ibid 118.

12 Ibid 120.

13 Phillippa C Diedrichs and Christina Lee, 'Waif Goodbye! Average-Size Female Models Promote Positive Body Image and Appeal to Consumers' (2011) 26(10) *Psychology & Health* 1273, 1277.

14 Ibid 1286.

15 House of Commons, Women and Equalities, *Changing the Perfect Picture: An Inquiry into Body Image* (Report No HC 274, 9 April 2021) <https://committees.parliament.uk/publications/5357/documents/53751/default/>.

improve social media so it harms body image less and presented their recommendations at the Australian Federal Parliament.[16] Butterfly Foundation is a national charity for Australians who are impacted by body image challenges and eating disorders and the people who support them.[17] Butterfly Foundation gives evidence-based assistance, resources and treatment.[18] One of the recommendations was that the Federal Government creates legislation that requires social media advertisements to show images with people who have diverse appearances (e.g. body shapes, sizes).[19] This further supports the idea that advertisers should use advertisements that show diverse women's bodies.

Showing Unedited Images Next to Edited Images

Researchers found that showing an image of the thin-ideal next to a natural, unedited image of the same person did not harm the viewer's body satisfaction as much as just showing the thin-ideal image.[20] Showing the images together can remind viewers that the thin-ideal is not realistic and the viewer should not compare themselves to it.[21] Displaying unedited images next to edited images may be difficult to implement because the people who post the images may be weary of the comments that they may receive.[22]

Exposure to Body Positive Content

Body positive content encourages people to accept their bodies as they are,[23] can be visual or written[24] and supports accepting all bodies, regardless of shape, appearance or size, including cellulite, etc.[25] It also challenges the thin-ideal.[26]

16 Butterfly Foundation and Zoe Daniel M.P., *Social Media, Body Image and Eating Disorders* (2024) <https://butterfly.org.au/wp-content/uploads/2024/05/Roundtable-Recommendations-FINAL-ONLINE.pdf>.

17 Butterfly Foundation, 'About Us' <https://butterfly.org.au/who-we-are/about-butterfly/>.

18 Ibid.

19 Ibid.

20 Marika Tiggemann and Isabella Anderberg, 'Social Media Is Not Real: The Effect of "Instagram vs Reality" Images on Women's Social Comparison and Body Image' (2020) 22(12) *New Media & Society* 2183, 2183–2198.

21 Ibid 2194.

22 Laura Vandenbosch, Jasmine Fardouly and Marika Tiggemann, 'Social Media and Body Image: Recent Trends and Future Directions' (2022) 45 *Current Opinion in Psychology* 1, 3.

23 Alexandra Sastre, 'Towards a Radical Body Positive: Reading the Online "Body Positive Movement"' (2014) 14(6) *Feminist Media Studies* 929, 929.

24 Jessica Cwynar-Horta, 'The Commodification of the Body Positive Movement on Instagram' *Stream: Culture/Politics/Technology* 36, 38.

25 Ibid.

26 Sastre (n 23) 929.

Researchers found that seeing body positive images can help body image. A study of 122 Italian women in their 20s found that daily exposure to body-positive images was associated with positive mood and body satisfaction.[27] A limitation of the study is that only young Italian women participated and the results may not apply to other countries and cultures.[28]

A survey of 192 women and transgender women between the ages of 19 and 77 saw messages and photographs supporting thin bodies, athletic bodies, curvy bodies or all types of bodies, called 'body-acceptance' messages.[29] Participants preferred the 'body-acceptance' messages. More educated participants less preferred the messages associated with thin bodies, which could be because they applied critical thinking skills they learned while in university.[30]

> Exposure to athletic messages yielded the worst outcomes in terms of self-objectification and body image. Seeing larger or stronger women in the pages of a magazine may feel novel or even hopeful, but this does not seem to translate into positive outcomes for women's body image. To the contrary, women may be especially vulnerable to messages promoting the curvy or athletic body-ideal, because they may not be able to recognize the drawbacks of those messages. In particular, the athletic ideal may be confounded with messages about maintaining good health, even as they promote a very specific body-ideal that is unattainable for most women. The disconnect between women's attitudes toward these messages and the consequences for body image and self-objectification are worthy of intervention.[31]

Another study by the same researchers, of 188 female and one gender fluid person who were mostly university students in the United States aged 18 to 62, involved the study participants watching one of four types of messages related to bodies that were used in the first study ((i) thin, (ii) athletic, (iii) curvy, (iv) 'body-acceptance'). The participants then saw a slideshow of the messages with images and the researchers evaluated their body image afterwards.[32] The researchers found that seeing the athletic messages had the worst

27 Giulia Fioravanti et al, 'Examining the Impact of Daily Exposure to Body-Positive and Fitspiration Instagram Content on Young Women's Mood and Body Image: An Intensive Longitudinal Study' (2023) 25(12) *New Media & Society* 3266, 3275–3276, 3281–3281.

28 Ibid 3283.

29 Diana E Betz and Laura R Ramsey, 'Should Women Be "All About That Bass?": Diverse Body-Ideal Messages and Women's Body Image' (2017) 22 *Body Image* 18, 20.

30 Ibid 23.

31 Ibid 28.

32 Ibid 25.

impact on their body image.[33] The curvy images did not harm the participants' body image,[34] nor did the 'body-acceptance' messages and images.[35]

An Australian study of 159 young adult women aged 18–25 who live in Australia involved giving 49 participants positive body image content to see on Facebook. Participants were also assigned to the 'appearance neutral' Facebook group and the control group.[36] Researchers took the body positive content from popular body positive social media pages, with the permission of the content creators.[37] Over 14 days, seeing a small number of body positive posts decreased women's body dissatisfaction and their appearance comparison.[38] The control group did not change.[39] The effects from viewing the body positive and body neutral posts continued for a month after the study.[40]

Not Digitally Altering Photos

In January 2014, staff of Aerie, a large American lingerie company that promotes its products to teenage girls, created the Aerie Real campaign that used images that were not digitally altered.[41] A study compared the impact of 200 first- or second-year female undergraduate students seeing images from the Aerie Real campaign to images from a previous Aerie campaign where the images were digitally altered.[42] They found that for study participants who did not frequently compare their appearance to others there was no difference between seeing the Aerie Real images and the modified images from prior Aerie campaigns. For study participants with high levels of appearance comparison, seeing Aerie Real images was 'less detrimental' to their body satisfaction compared to study participants who saw images from prior Aerie campaigns.[43] Researchers also found that not digitally altering models' images harmed the body satisfaction of some young women and other businesses less than showing them digitally altered images: they suggested other businesses should act similarly.[44] Also, the study participants' desire to buy

33 Ibid 26–27.

34 Ibid 27.

35 Ibid.

36 Jasmine Fardouly et al, 'Can Following Body Positive or Appearance Neutral Facebook Pages Improve Young Women's Body Image and Mood? Testing Novel Social Media Micro-Interventions' (2023) 44 *Body Image* 136, 138.

37 Ibid 140.

38 Ibid 145.

39 Ibid 142–143.

40 Ibid 144.

41 Alexandra D Convertino et al, 'An Evaluation of the Aerie Real Campaign: Potential for Promoting Positive Body Image?' (2019) 24(6) *Journal of Health Psychology* 726, 726–727.

42 Ibid 728.

43 Ibid 734.

44 Ibid 734.

the product advertised did not change depending on whether they saw modified or non-modified images.[45]

Reality Check Comments

A small amount of research found that viewing positive appearance comments plus 'reality check' comments results in less body dissatisfaction than just viewing body positive comments.[46] 'Reality check' comments are statements that challenge what viewers see in an image, for example, if someone wrote 'this is not realistic' under a thin-ideal image.[47]

Rewarding Businesses That Use Models Who Appear to Have Healthy Bodies

As Chapter 5 previously discussed, Yvan Baker (a Member of the Provincial Parliament of Ontario, Canada, at the time) proposed a bill in the Legislative Assembly of Ontario, Canada, that included creating awards and giving them to businesses that try to lower the number of people with eating disorders.[48] The Australian National Advisory Group on Body Image, which created the Voluntary Industry Code of Conduct on Body Image,[49] also recommended creating awards to give businesses that support the Code. Award winners could be spokespeople who promote positive body image in their industry and their business could be used as a case study to show the commercial benefits from acting in ways that are positive for body image. It also encouraged the Federal Government to sponsor the awards.[50]

The awards were given in 2012, and again in 2013 (that year a health and well-being industry category was added). The winners could show a Positive Body Image Award Symbol in their advertising. In 2012, *Dolly* magazine won the award because it promoted positive body image to young people. Among other positive body image actions it took were that it had a policy not to manipulate images and to present images of young women who were not models nor the thin-ideal. In 2013 fashion clothing store chain Sportsgirl won

45 Ibid 735.

46 Marika Tiggemann and Vasiliki Georgia Velissaris, 'The Effect of Viewing Challenging "Reality Check" Instagram Comments on Women's Body Image' (2020) 33 *Body Image* 257, 261.

47 Ibid 258.

48 *Combatting Eating Disorders in Ontario Act, 2018,* Bill 29, 41st Leg, 3rd Sess, Ontario, 2018, s 6.

49 Australian Government, 'Voluntary Industry Code of Conduct on Body Image' <http://www.mediaknite.org/wp-content/uploads/2016/07/Body-Image-code-of-conduct.pdf>.

50 National Advisory Group on Body Image, *A Proposed National Strategy on Body Image* (Commonwealth of Australia, 2009) <https://www.eatingdisorderhope.com/pdf/Proposed-National-Strategy-on-Body-Image_australia.pdf>.

the award for their policies that supported positive body image and selling clothes in diverse sizes.[51]

In the United Kingdom, in 2012, the British Government, through the Campaign for Body Confidence, gave Body Confidence Awards to businesses, advocates and celebrities who took measures to try to improve body image. Dove received an award for promoting body positivity to girls and pharmacy Boots won for not retouching images.[52]

The author hopes that by governments giving these awards to businesses that took actions that were positive for body image, consumers would then decide to further shop at these businesses. In turn, this could encourage the businesses to continue these efforts and other businesses to act similarly. This is a business measure to try to improve body image, not a legal one. To try to improve body image and lower the number of people who have eating disorders, measures from several disciplines (e.g. business, psychology, public health) are necessary. Also, sometimes when a problem may appear to require legal assistance, it could be better served with a business solution with no legal intervention entirely.

Measures Involving Tax

'The tax system may offer our strongest and most viable policy options to discourage the use of digitally altered images'.[53] This book previously described a bill that did not pass, in Massachusetts, United States, to give tax credits of a $10,000 (U.S.) maximum to businesses that do not alter images of models.[54]

There are examples of governments giving businesses a tax credit to encourage them to act in ways that are good for society, for example, the Small Business Health Care Tax Credit in the United States, which gives a tax credit to small businesses that pay for at least 50% of their employees' health care coverage.[55]

Governments could also create a direct tax on using digitally altered advertisements, so advertisers would stop digitally altering advertisements to avoid

51 Paxton (n 2) 663.

52 Ibid 664.

53 Monica Kriete, *Regulating Digitally Manipulated Advertising in the United States to Prevent Eating Disorders* (Policy Brief, Strategic Training Initiative for the Prevention of Eating Disorders, November 2018) <https://hsph.harvard.edu/wp-content/uploads/2024/11/Altered-Images-Policy-Brief.pdf>.

54 Commonwealth of Massachusetts, An Act Relative to Mental Health Promotion through Realistic Advertising Images, House Bill H 2860, § 1.

55 Internal Revenue Service, 'Small Business Health Care Tax Credit and the SHOP Marketplace' (Web Page, 30 September 2024) <https://www.irs.gov/affordable-care-act/employers/small-business-health-care-tax-credit-and-the-shop-marketplace>.

paying the tax.[56] If a government creates a direct tax, advertisers might decide to pay the tax instead of ceasing to digitally alter their advertisements.[57] A direct tax would need to be a meaningful amount so that it would have a decent chance to deter businesses from breaching the law, like an appropriate percentage of revenue, or a suitable percentage of another type of fiscal measure so that it is consequential and fair to both smaller and larger businesses.

The Need to Change the Culture within Industry

Researchers in the United Kingdom conducted qualitative, semi-structured interviews with people who work in senior leadership positions in the beauty, advertising and fashion industries (over 80% were women).[58] The researchers chose the participants through finding businesses associated with positive body image and people whose work involved positive body image measures (e.g. not digitally modifying models' bodies).[59] The women stated that their own connection to body image inspired them to want to undertake body image-related work.[60] Many of them stated that their clients, superiors and others held negative views of models in larger bodies, so they do not employ them as models.

One study participant stated clients do not let them put people with larger bodies in advertisements.[61] They also believed that it would be easier to take positive body image-related actions if more businesses did.[62] They further asserted that it was hard to implement measures relating to positive body image when other stakeholders opposed it (e.g. photographers, casting directors).[63] They added that the majority of people in power in the pertinent industries were white males, which they thought made it more difficult to take body positive measures, and they felt that women in power were more likely to support positive body image work. They also believed that implementing positive body image measures could help to create a competitive advantage and result in positive media coverage and influencer posts.[64] The participants believed that taking positive body image actions would be profitable, but only over the

56 Caitlin McBride et al, 'Digital Manipulation of Images of Models' Appearance in Advertising: Strategies for Action through Law and Corporate Social Responsibility Incentives to Protect Public Health' (2019) 45 *American Journal of Law & Medicine* 7, 20–21.

57 Ibid 26.

58 Nadia Craddock et al, 'Can Big Business Foster Positive Body Image? Qualitative Insights from Industry Leaders Walking the Talk' (2019) 30 *Body Image* 93, 95.

59 Ibid 96.

60 Ibid 98.

61 Ibid 99.

62 Ibid 101.

63 Ibid.

64 Ibid 102.

long term. They added that they thought that if a business took a short-term or one-off view of body image, then this could result in public backlash.[65] This research (and research from earlier in this chapter) indicates that it could be helpful to educate people in the beauty, advertising and fashion industries on the thin-ideal and how viewing it can harm some people. It may be additionally useful to inform them of the research that found that using images of models who are not the thin-ideal can still be very effective. This may result in people who work in those industries enacting measures that are helpful for body image without legislation compelling them to.

Conclusion

This chapter mostly discussed various measures that could help to improve body image. After considering all of these options, it is important to consider which, if any, should become Body Image Law. That is, which of them should turn into a law that would hopefully result in less thin-ideal images existing and/or these images having less of a negative impact on body image and be less likely to contribute to developing eating disorders.

This raises (at least) two important questions: (1) which of the options is most likely to help improve body image?; and (2) which is most feasible as legislation? To become a Body Image Law, a measure should satisfy both. Relevantly, not every good idea (no matter how much it can help people) can become legislation; a multitude of constraints can prevent it (which the conclusion to this chapter will discuss soon).

In terms of which option is most likely to help to improve body image, regrettably, the answer appears unknown currently, because most do not have much research to support them and as stated previously, the author takes an evidence-based approach. Using diverse bodies in images and displaying body positive content appear to have a good amount of research to support them as measures that can help body image. The author found a paucity of research relating to showing unedited images next to edited images and not digitally altering images. She found no research pertaining to the impact of the following measures in the body image context: rewarding businesses that use models who appear to have healthy bodies, and tax measures.

Regarding which of the measures is most likely to be feasible as legislation, unfortunately, this, too, is difficult to say. To start, each country has its own unique constitution (if it has a constitution) and its own existing legislation. A constitution is a country's most important piece of legislation and other legislation cannot breach it. Moreover, the constitution, or other legislation, may give a government powers to make legislation and/or set limits on it.

65 Ibid 103.

So, a government would need to have the power to create a Body Image Law and not have a limit on its ability to.

Further, a law that might be possible to pass in one country might be impossible to pass in another, or the government might pass a law only for it to be challenged in court and then deemed unconstitutional (for example, because the law breaches that particular country's constitution or its bill of rights). It follows that a researcher must examine whether a Body Image Law is legally feasible by assessing it within the context of the particular country. The author nevertheless believes that generally creating a law that forbids digitally altering images should be legally feasible, although it would not be identical in every country. The tax options are also likely legally feasible. To start, tax credits and tax cuts are common measures in many countries and federal parliaments usually have the power to charge a tax or give a tax credit: politicians could possibly use existing tax law as a basis for a tax-related Body Image Law.

The author recommends that more research takes place about some of the potential measures to improve body image, and then legal feasibility is assessed of the measures that appear to help most. Also, the author recommends considering the possibility of a Body Image Law with a few different parts, if there is evidence to support the effectiveness of each.

Regardless of how any Body Image Law is created or amended, any policy or regulation relating to eating disorders must be evaluated[66] (and so should any law, policy or regulation generally) to see if it is effective, and if it is not, politicians should modify it, repeal it, etc.

66 S Bryn Austin, 'A Public Health Approach to Eating Disorders Prevention: It's Time for Public Health Professionals to Take a Seat at the Table' (2012) 12(1) *BMC Public Health* 1, 5.

9 Conclusion

Introduction

The introduction to this book, and indeed, its opening sentence, said that the current state of Body Image Law appears to be 'a dogs' breakfast'. After thoroughly considering the research in this area perhaps it might be said, at least, that part of Body Image Law appears problematic: that which requires disclaimers on images of models whose bodies were digitally altered. It appears more appropriate to call the rest of Body Image Law a hopeful question mark, because it is relatively new, deserves further research and has potential to help many.

Key Findings from This Book

This book makes several key findings. Many researchers found that when some women see thin-ideal images, this may result in them experiencing poor body image and developing eating disorders. Addressing this problem relates to the aim of Body Image Law: to create law and/or policy so that there are less thin-ideal images and/or that these images have a smaller negative impact on body image and are less likely to contribute to developing eating disorders. Also, viewing social media can negatively impact body image: it has a ubiquitous number of thin-ideal images.

Body Image Law, as it currently exists, in its written form and in the real world, seems to be a hodgepodge of legislation, bills and policy internationally, and may not be achieving its aims. However, the author reminds you of the study, mentioned in Chapter 5, on the impact of the Israeli Body Image Law, about eight years after it came into effect,[1] that found that it caused about 26% of the younger study participants to say that it moderately changed their beliefs about the thin-ideal.[2] This is rare evidence to support that Body Image

1 See Michal Cohen and Yael Latzer, 'The Impact of Israel's "Models' Law" on Young Women' (2021) 13(4) *International Journal of Psychological Studies* 32, 32.

2 Ibid 43–44.

DOI: 10.4324/9781003678793-9

Law may be effective, but it is far from conclusive evidence that Body Image Law is definitely effective and in all its conceivable forms.

There are different options to consider to help address the harm that seeing thin-ideal images can cause, that could potentially form the basis of a Body Image Law or part thereof. They are: using models with diverse bodies in images, showing unedited images next to edited images of models, displaying body positive content, not digitally altering any images, rewarding businesses that take positive action regarding body image and implementing a tax. There are differing amounts of research related to each option, but overall, there is little research about most of them. One or more used simultaneously may be an effective way to address the problem at hand. More research should occur before advocating for this takes place.

This book also discussed the health challenges that models face and argued that politicians should broaden the aims of Body Image Law so that the health of models becomes part thereof. If a model's health improves, their body may then look less like the thin-ideal, which could result in less thin-ideal images (one of Body Image Law's original aims). Another key finding from this book is that if Body Image Laws are to be effective, the support of affected industries is critical to increase the chances that people will abide by the law.

Additionally, Pro-Ana content on social media, which encourages people to develop eating disorders, can harm the people who view it. The French Government did not pass its proposed legislation that would have resulted in fining and imprisoning people who create Pro-Ana material online. Politicians should not create legislation that punishes the person who produced Pro-Ana content, because commonly they have an eating disorder and engaging with the criminal justice system could worsen it. People with eating disorders deserve support and compassion, not a jail sentence. Instead, if politicians legislate this issue, the legislation should require social media to prevent this kind of content from appearing and remove it promptly if it appears: this would likely be more helpful, practical and just.

The Future of Body Image and Eating Disorders

It is relevant to consider the future of body image and eating disorders, and politicians should be prepared to modify Body Image Law, where appropriate, to reflect changes.

One important aspect of the future of body image and eating disorders is Ozempic, medication that reduces hunger and makes people feel full.[3] The American Food and Drug Administration approved Semaglutide for weight

3 Gemma Sharp et al, 'New Anti-Obesity Medications: Considerations and Future Directions in People with Concurrent Eating Disorders' (2023) 52(9) *Australian Journal of General Practice* 651, 651.

loss in 2021.[4] Semaglutide is the active ingredient in Ozempic.[5] There is concern that people with eating disorders will use the medication, without a prescription.[6] There is currently a paucity of research about how Ozempic can impact eating disorders, though there is some that states that Ozempic could potentially 'cause, maintain or worsen' eating disorders.[7] Ozempic use, and the recent increase of thin-ideal models,[8] may make considering (and maybe also passing) Body Image Law more relevant than ever, because there may be even more thin-ideal models (because they use Ozempic) and accordingly, more images of them for the public to see. Further, many celebrities with larger bodies are now becoming thin, which may result in there being less diverse bodies in the mainstream media. There may also be more thin-ideal people in the world, generally. Most are not models and Body Image Law's purview does not extend to the bodies of people who are not featured in the public domain.

Another aspect of the future of eating disorders involves its diagnosis. Recently, clinicians, researchers and people who have eating disorders, from 13 countries, developed a way to measure whether a person has an eating disorder that could be applied uniformly, the Eating Disorder Set.[9] If clinicians adopt it internationally, then politicians may want to consider whether the Body Image Laws that include a model needing to fulfil certain criteria to work (e.g. the Israeli and French Body Image Laws) should be modified to include the Eating Disorder Set criteria. This would align with the recommendation that the aim of the Body Image Laws is broadened to consider the health of the models.

Many eating disorder clinicians use artificial intelligence in their practice in a way that involves treating eating disorders (although cautiously): they most commonly use ChatGPT.[10] Artificial intelligence can offer resources to

4 Food and Drug Administration, 'FDA Approves New Drug Treatment for Chronic Weight Management, First Since 2014' (Media Release, 4 June 2021) <https://www.fda.gov/news-events/press-announcements/fda-approves-new-drug-treatment-chronic-weight-management-first-2014>.

5 European Medicines Agency, 'Ozempic' (Web Page, 21 February 2018) <https://www.ema.europa.eu/en/medicines/human/EPAR/ozempic>.

6 Sharp et al (n 3) 651.

7 Sara Bartel et al, 'Use of Glucagon-like Peptide-1 Receptor Agonists in Eating Disorder Populations' (2024) 57(2) *The International Journal of Eating Disorders* 286, 290.

8 Chloe Mac Donnell, 'Fashion Experts Raise Concern about Return to "Extremely Thin Models"', *The Guardian* (online, 11 October 2024) <https://www.theguardian.com/fashion/2024/oct/11/fashion-experts-raise-concern-about-return-to-using-extremely-thin-models>.

9 Amelia Austin et al, 'International Consensus on Patient-Centred Outcomes in Eating Disorders' (2023) 10(12) *The Lancet Psychiatry* 966, 968, 971.

10 Jake Lindardon et al, 'Current Practices and Perspectives of Artificial Intelligence in the Clinical Management of Eating Disorders: Insights From Clinicians and Community Participants' [2025] *The International Journal of Eating Disorders* 1, 8.

people who have eating disorders 24 hours a day, seven days a week, which can supplement what clinicians tell them. It can comment on food diaries, give encouragement and modify client records and case notes.[11]

Artificial intelligence chatbots are also currently being used to provide information about eating disorders.[12] At this point in time, the longer and more complex a conversation is with a chatbot, the more likely it is that there will be errors in the information that it provides.[13] The California Body Image Law, which legislates giving eating disorder and nutrition information to models,[14] may be relevant. Perhaps artificial intelligence can help to inform models about these and similar topics, which aligns with the suggested new goal of Body Image Law, to improve models' health.

There may also be issues involving artificial intelligence when advertisers use it to create images in advertisements that are not actually humans, but look like them, to sell products. People use artificial intelligence to create increasing numbers of fake models: some of these models have millions of followers.[15] Some businesses even solely use models that artificial intelligence created.[16] Denim retailer Levi Strauss uses artificial intelligence, though it faced a backlash[17] which did not stop it from continuing to do so.[18] The H&M clothing store chain announced that it will use artificial intelligence to create images of models which look like them: 'twins'.[19] If models give it permission, then H&M will use a model's 'twin' instead of the model in images and pay the model for doing so. H&M will initially only use the 'twins' in their social media and add a watermark on the image to clarify that they used artificial intelligence to make it.[20]

In terms of using artificial intelligence to create models and Body Image Law, when this occurs, the part of Body Image Law that requires human models to have a minimum BMI or to obtain a medical certificate or similar would

11 Ibid 9–10.

12 Gemma Sharp, John Torous and Madeline L West, 'Ethical Challenges in AI Approaches to Eating Disorders' (2023) 25(1) *Journal of Medical Internet Research* 1, 1.

13 William W Chan et al, 'The Challenges in Designing a Prevention Chatbot for Eating Disorders: Observational Study' (2022) 6(1) *JMIR Formative Research* 1, 10.

14 Assembly Bill 2338, Talent Protections Act, 2017 – 18 Reg Sess, California, 2018 § 1700.51.

15 Leisa Scott and Rebecca Armstrong, 'How Modelling Agent Chelsea Bonner Is Taking on Artificial Intelligence to Avoid "Cataclysmic Step Backwards for Industry"', *ABC* (online, 6 May 2024) <https://www.abc.net.au/news/2024-05-06/chelsea-bonner-fight-against-ai-models/103769766>.

16 Ibid.

17 Alaina Demopoulos, 'Computer-Generated Inclusivity: Fashion Turns to "Diverse" AI Models', *The Guardian* (online, 3 April 2023) <https://www.theguardian.com/fashion/2023/apr/03/ai-virtual-models-fashion-brands>.

18 Liv McMahon, 'H&M to Use Digital Clones of Models in Ads and Social Media', *BBC* (online, 27 March 2025) <https://www.bbc.com/news/articles/c3vwg73xndeo>.

19 Ibid.

20 Ibid.

be irrelevant (because no human model is involved). One potential way to modify Body Image Law to apply to images that artificial intelligence creates would be to state that using artificial intelligence to create a model to use in an advertisement is illegal. Given how much cheaper it is to use artificial intelligence to create a model than to use a real one,[21] it would be challenging to convince people to abide by it. If brands use artificial intelligence to create models, then not only would they likely not need to pay models (though H&M does[22]), but they would not need to pay the creative people who work in associated industries, such as hair, makeup and lighting.[23] Another possibility is to create requirements for what the models in the images that artificial intelligence created need to look like – general or specific measurements. It could also include requirements that relate to diversity among the models in a single image.

As well, lawmakers could modify Body Image Law to require a disclaimer on advertisements with models that artificial intelligence made that states that artificial intelligence created them and they do not feature real humans or a variation thereof. This is a similar idea to H&M's decision to add a watermark on images that use models that artificial intelligence made.[24] It is also similar to the French Influencer Law, passed in 2023, that this book earlier discussed, which stated that if an influencer uses artificial intelligence to create a face or silhouette, it must have the phrase 'virtual image'.[25] Since disclaimers on images that were digitally altered to make models look thinner are ineffective,[26] the author questions whether the French law requiring

21 Brooke Kato, 'Fashion Models Step aside as AI Glam Bots Join Them in Ads: "It's about Faster Content Creation"', *New York Post* (online, 31 October 2024) <https://nypost.com/2024/10/31/lifestyle/fashion-models-pushed-to-the-side-as-ai-glam-bots-take-over/>.

22 McMahon (n 18).

23 Lauren Cochrane, 'Calling all Fashion Models…Now AI Is Coming For You', *The Guardian* (online, 31 March 2025) <https://www.theguardian.com/fashion/2025/mar/30/fashion-models-ai-job-losses>.

24 McMahon (n 18).

25 *Loi no 2023-451 du juin 2023 visant à encadrer l'influence commerciale et à lutter contre les dérives des influenceurs sur les réseaux sociaux* (France) JO, 10 juin 2023, no 0133, texte no 1, s 2, art 5 II(2).

26 Z Brown and M Tiggemann, 'A Picture Is Worth a Thousand Words: The Effect of Viewing Celebrity Instagram Images with Disclaimer and Body Positive Captions on Women's Body Image' (2020) (33) *Body Image* 190, 195; Francesca Giorgianni, Elisa Danthinne and Rachel F Rodgers, 'Consumer Warning versus Systemic Change: The Effects of Including Disclaimer Labels on Images That Have or Have Not Been Digitally Modified on Body Image' (2020) 34 *Body Image* 249, 255; Nehama Lewis, Ayellet Pelled and Nurit Tal-Or, 'The Effect of Exposure to Thin Models and Digital Modification Disclaimers on Women's Body Satisfaction' (2020) 55(2) *International Journal of Psychology* 245, 250; Julianne Livingston, Elise Holland and Jasmine Fardouly, 'Exposing Digital Posing: The Effect of Social Media Self-Disclaimer Captions on Women's Body Dissatisfaction, Mood, and Impressions of the User' (2020) 32 *Body Image* 150, 153.

the disclaimer on images that artificial intelligence made would be effective in relation to the body image of viewers. Further research on this issue could be useful, especially considering the recent increasing use of artificial intelligence.

Chapter 4 of this book discussed some American lawsuits involving litigants suing social media for contributing to their eating disorders. The outcome of this litigation is important: if the plaintiffs are successful it could provide useful precedent for similar lawsuits in the future relating to Pro-Ana content in the United States, and possibly be persuasive judgments for judicial officers in other countries. However, the majority of litigation settles before a trial, so it is conceivable that no judgment will be handed down for these cases.

Concluding Remarks

This book considered Body Image Law comprehensively through the lens of evidence, without rose-coloured glasses. The author hopes, moving forward, that politicians will do the same, to try to create the best outcome.

Whilst the author frequently uses the word 'hope' and variations of it in relation to Body Image Law, this is unfortunate, because hope is often associated with uncertainty. Uncertain, though, is perhaps a more appropriate adjective for Body Image Law at this point in time and likely sounds better than the phrase 'a dog's breakfast'. There is reason to hope: in particular, the evidence in Chapter 8 about the measures that could improve body image provides practical ways to consider a future where there are less thin-ideal images or they are less harmful.

Significant 'large-scale' population health change has occurred internationally for other challenges, such as tobacco use, seat belt and helmet use: the same could happen to prevent eating disorders,[27] with Body Image Law playing a part in it.

'Almost every girl grows up wanting to be beautiful'.[28] For some girls, and women, this desire can, at some point, result in psychological and physical harm, like an eating disorder. How wonderful would it be if no girl grew up wanting to be beautiful. If they wanted to grow up to be caring, thoughtful, smart and ambitious instead.

The first chapter of this book stated that if there is one thing that the author hopes that this book accomplishes for you it is this: to make you contemplate

27 Megan Jones Bell, Rachel F Rodgers and Susan J Paxton, 'Towards Successful Evidence-Based Universal Eating Disorders Prevention: The Importance of Zooming Out' (2017) 25 *Eating Behaviors: An International Journal* 89, 91.

28 Cassandra A Soltis, 'Dying to Be a Supermodel: Can Requiring a Healthy BMI Be Fashionable?' (2010) 26 *Journal of Contemporary Health Law and Policy* 49, 49.

(if you have not already) that the thin-ideal is an artificial concept that you should not try to aspire to, nor expect anyone else to. The author reminds you of this aspiration, and genuinely hopes that it stays with you long after you finish this book.

This book occasionally and importantly thought about the future, and the author will end it by doing so (or end this part of the book, before the Annexures).

She asks you to think about the next generation of girls and women, and the generation after them, and hope that with research, critical thinking, tremendous, well-targeted advocacy, comprehensive education and making body image and eating disorders a legislative priority, *future girls and women never try to change their bodies to conform to artificial notions of beauty*. Instead, it's merely something that they can read about in history and similar books (if they choose to). #BodyImageLaw:RevolutionisingImagesOfThinIdealWomen? #ThanksForReading #LaFin

Annexures

Annexure A A List of All Body Image Law Internationally, as at 3 March 2025

Jurisdiction	*Is It a Bill, Law or Policy?*	*Title of the Bill, Law or Policy*	*If It Was a Law, What Year Did It Pass?*
Australia	Policy	*Voluntary Industry Code of Conduct on Body Image*	
Brazil	Bill	*Projeto De Lei N.º 6.853-B, De 2010* [Bill No. 6,853-B, 2010] (Brazil), 24 February 2010	
Canada – Ontario	Bill	*Combatting Eating Disorders in Ontario Act, 2018,* Bill 29, 41st Leg, 3rd Sess, Ontario, 2018	
Canada – Quebec	Policy	*Quebec Charter for a Healthy and Diverse Body Image*	
Denmark	Policy	*Danish Fashion Ethical Charter*	
France	Bill	*Proposition de loi relative aux photographies d'images corporelles retouchées* [Proposed Law on Retouched Body Image Photographs] (France), 15 September 2009, N° 1908	
France	Law	*Code de la santé publique* [Public Health Code] (France)	Passed in 2017
France	Law	*Code du travail* [Labour Code] (France)	Passed in 2017
France	Law	*Loi no 2023-451 du juin 2023 visant à encadrer l'influence commerciale et à lutter contre les dérives des influenceurs sur les réseaux sociaux* (France) JO, 10 juin 2023, no 0133	Passed in 2023

(*Continued*)

Annexure A (Continued)

Jurisdiction	*Is It a Bill, Law or Policy?*	*Title of the Bill, Law or Policy*	*If It Was a Law, What Year Did It Pass?*
Israel	Law	הצעת חוק הגבלת משקל בענף הדוגמנות [Law for Restricting Weight in the Modelling Industry], 27 March 2012, 5772-2012	Passed in 2012
Israel	Law	הצעת חוק הגבלת משקל בענף הדוגמנות תיקון הוראות שונות [Law for Restricting Weight in the Modelling Industry] (Amendment – Various Provisions), 2 September 2022, 5776-2016 (P/2825/20)	Did not pass
Italy – Milan	Policy	No specific title found – policy involved models needing to have a minimum BMI to walk on the runway	
Norway	Law	*Lov Om Endringer i Markedsføringsloven mv. (Merking Av Retusjert Reklame)* [Act on Amendments to the Marketing Act, etc. (Labelling of Retouched Advertising)] (Norway), 11 June 2021, No. 62	Passed in 2021
Spain – Madrid	Policy	No specific title found – policy involved a minimum BMI for models to walk on the runway	
United Kingdom	Bill	*Digitally Altered Body Images Bill 2019* (U.K.)	
United Kingdom – London	Policy	*Transport for London's Advertising Policy*	
United States – Arizona	Bill	House Bill 2793, An Act Requiring Disclaimers on Digitally Altered Advertising Images, 50th Leg, 2nd Reg Sess (Ariz, 2012)	
United States – California	Bill	Assembly Bill 2539, An Act to Add Section 1812.610 to the Civil Code, Relating to Employment of Models, 2015–16 Reg Sess, California, 2016	
United States – California	Law	Assembly Bill 2338, Talent Protections Act, 2017–18 Reg Sess, California, 2018 § 1700.50	Passed in 2018
United States – Massachusetts	Bill	Commonwealth of Massachusetts, An Act Relative to Mental Health Promotion through Realistic Advertising Images, House Bill H 2860	Did not pass

Annexure B List of Advertising Self-Regulators' Rulings Related to Body Image (That the Author Could Find)

Jurisdiction	*Citation*	*Advertising Self-Regulator's Decision*
Australia	*The Good Foundation* (2019, Ad Standards Community Panel, 0097/19) <https://adstandards.com.au/wp-content/uploads /2023/08/0097-19.pdf>.	Dismissed
Australia	*Health Products* (2019, Ad Standards Community Panel, 0550/18) <https://adstandards.com.au/wp-content/uploads/2023/08 /0550-18.pdf>.	Dismissed
New Zealand	*AA Insurance Print and Digital Marketing* (2024, ASA NZ, 24/094) <https://asa.co.nz /decision /24-094-aa-insurance-print-and-digital-marketing/>.	Settled (Ad Removed/Amended)
New Zealand	*Les Mills Israel, Facebook* (2025, ASA NZ, 25/047) <https://asa.co.nz/decision/25-047-les-mills-israel-facebook/>.	No Jurisdiction
New Zealand	*Woolworths NZ* (2024, ASA NZ, 24/182) <https://asa.co.nz /decision/24-182-woolworths-nz-milkrun-email/>.	Settled (Ad Removed/ Amended)
United Kingdom	*ASA Ruling on Aestheal Clinic* (2025, ASA UK, A23-1199874) <https://www.asa.org.uk/rulings /aestheal-clinic-a23-1199874 -aestheal-clinic.html>.	Upheld
United Kingdom	*ASA Ruling on Aspro Atlantic Medikal Turizm Ticaret Limited Sirketi T/A AsproMED* (2023, ASA UK, A23-1199868) <https://www.asa.org.uk/rulings/aspro -atlantic-medikal-turizm-ticaret -limited-irketi.html>.	Upheld
United Kingdom	*ASA Ruling on Beautyjenics* (2025, ASA UK, A25-1274802) <https://www.asa.org.uk/rulings/beautyjenics-ltd-a25-1274802 -beautyjenics-ltd.html>.	Upheld

(*Continued*)

Annexure B (Continued)

Jurisdiction	*Citation*	*Advertising Self-Regulator's Decision*
United Kingdom	*ASA Ruling on CCskinlondondubai* (2025, ASA UK, A25-1274786) <https://www.asa.org.uk/rulings/ccskinlondondubai-a25-1274786-ccskinlondondubai.html>.	Upheld
United Kingdom	*ASA Ruling on Dakik Saglik Medikal Turizm A.S. T/A Clincexpert Hospital* (2023, ASA UK, A23-1199876) <https://www.asa.org.uk/rulings/dakik-saglik-medikal-turizm-a-s--a23-1199876-clinicexpert.html>.	Upheld
United Kingdom	*ASA Ruling on Egemed Hastaneleri* (2025, ASA UK, A22-1178817) <https://www.asa.org.uk/rulings/egemed-hastaneleri-a22-1178817-egemed-hospitals.html>.	Upheld
United Kingdom	*ASA Ruling on Erdem Clinic* (2023, ASA United Kingdom, A23-1199873) <https://www.asa.org.uk/rulings/erdem-clinic-a23-1199873-erdem-clinic.html>.	Upheld
United Kingdom	*ASA Ruling on GM Unicorn Corporation Ltd* (2023, ASA UK, A22-1180376) <https://www.asa.org.uk/rulings/gm-unicorn-corporation-ltd-A22-1180376.html>.	Upheld
United Kingdom	*ASA Ruling on Grand Clinic* (2023, ASA UK, A23-1199864) <https://www.asa.org.uk/rulings/grand-clinic-a23-1199864-grand-clinic-html>.	Upheld

Annexure B (Continued)

Jurisdiction	*Citation*	*Advertising Self-Regulator's Decision*
United Kingdom	*ASA Ruling on Guangzhou YH Sporting Goods Co Ltd T/A Young&Healthy* (2022, ASA UK, G22-1153152) <https://www.asa.org.uk/rulings/guangzhou-yh-sporting-goods-co-ltd-g22-1153152-guangzhou-yh-sporting-goods-co-ltd.html>.	Upheld
United Kingdom	*ASA Ruling on Hongkong Jigao Technology Co Ltd t/a Chic Me* (2022, ASA UK, A22-1161867) <https://www.asa.org.uk/rulings/hongkong-jigao-technology-co-ltd-a22-1161867-hongkong-jigao-technology-co-ltd.html>.	Not Upheld
United Kingdom	*ASA Ruling on JA Physique Ltd T/A JakeAbbott07* (2022, ASA UK, A22-1155446) <https://www.asa.org.uk/rulings/ja-physique-ltd-a22-1155446-ja-physique-ltd.html>.	Upheld
United Kingdom	*ASA Ruling on Linia Cosmetic Surgery* (2022, ASA UK, A21-1136723) <https://www.asa.org.uk/rulings/linia-cosmetic-surgery-a21-1136723-linia-cosmetic-surgery.html>.	Upheld in Part
United Kingdom	*ASA Ruling on Maje SAS T/A Maje SAS* (2023, ASA UK, A23-1202525) <https://www.asa.org.uk/rulings/maje-sas-a23-1202525-maje-sas.html>.	Upheld
United Kingdom	*ASA Ruling on Pall Mall Medical (Manchester) Ltd T/A Pall Mall Cosmetics* (2024, ASA United Kingdom, A24-1252542) <https://www.asa.org.uk/rulings/pall-mall-medical--manchester--ltd-a24-1252542-pall-mall-medical--manchester--ltd.html>.	Upheld

(*Continued*)

Annexure B (Continued)

Jurisdiction	*Citation*	*Advertising Self-Regulator's Decision*
United Kingdom	*ASA Ruling on Persons Unknown* (2022, ASA UK, A22-1155620) <https://www.asa.org.uk/rulings/person-s--unknown-a22-1155620-person-s--unknown.html>.	Upheld
United Kingdom	*ASA Ruling on Sensilab D.O.O.* (2022, ASA UK, G22-1157038) <https://www.asa.org.uk/rulings/sensilab-d-o-o--g22-1157038-sensilab-d-o-o-.html>.	Upheld
United Kingdom	*ASA Ruling on Skinny Revolution Ltd* (2020, ASA UK, A20-1064728) <https://www.asa.org.uk/rulings/skinny-revolution-ltd-a20-1064728-skinny-revolution-ltd.html>.	Upheld
United Kingdom	*ASA Ruling on UAB Forma Perfecta T/A Fi Clinica* (2023, ASA UK, A23-1199866) <https://www.asa.org.uk/rulings/uab-forma-perfecta-a23-1199866-uab-forma-perfecta.html>.	Upheld
United Kingdom	*ASA Ruling on Unilever UK Ltd* (2023, ASA UK, G23-1203966) <https://www.asa.org.uk/rulings/unilever-uk-ltd-g23-1203966-unilever-uk-ltd.html>.	Not Upheld
United Kingdom	*ASA Ruling on WHM Hair Transplant and Aesthetics T/A WHM Clinic* (2023, ASA UK, A23-1199871) <https://www.asa.org.uk/rulings/whm-hair-transplant-and-aesthetics-a23-1199871-whm-hair-transplant-and-aesthetics.html>.	Upheld

Annexure C Social Media Community Guidelines on Eating Disorder Content

Social Media	*Policy Regarding Eating Disorder Content*
Meta	'We care deeply about the safety of the people who use our apps. We regularly consult with experts in suicide, self-injury and eating disorders to help inform our policies and enforcement, and we work with organisations around the world to provide assistance to people in distress. While we do not allow people to intentionally or unintentionally celebrate or promote suicide, self-injury or eating disorders, we do allow people to discuss these topics because we want our services to be a space where people can share their experiences, raise awareness about these issues and seek support from one another. We remove any content that encourages suicide, self-injury or eating disorders, including fictional content such as memes or illustrations and any self-injury content which is graphic, regardless of context. We also remove content that mocks victims or survivors of suicide, self-injury or eating disorders, as well as real-time depictions of suicide or self-injury. Content about recovery from suicide, self-injury or eating disorders that is allowed, but may contain imagery that could be upsetting (such as a healed scar) is placed behind a sensitivity screen. When people post or search for suicide-, self-injury- or eating disorders-related content, we will direct them to local organisations that can provide support and if our Community Operations team is concerned about immediate harm, we will contact local emergency services to get them help. For more information, visit the Meta Safety Centre… Do not post: Content that promotes, encourages, coordinates or provides instructions for suicide, self-injury or eating disorders. • Content that depicts graphic suicide, self-injury and eating disorder imagery… • Content that focuses on depiction of ribs, collar bones, thigh gaps, hips, concave stomach or protruding spine or scapula when shared together with terms associated with eating disorders • Content that contains instructions for drastic and unhealthy weight loss when shared together with terms associated with eating disorders • Content that mocks victims or survivors of suicide, self-injury or eating disorders who are either publicly known or implied to have experienced suicide or self-injury… For the following content, we include a label so that people are aware that the content may be sensitive:… • Content that depicts ribs, collar bones, thigh gaps, hips, concave stomach or protruding spine or scapula in a recovery context… We provide resources to people who post written or verbal admissions of engagement in self-injury, including:… • Eating disorders.[1]

[1] Meta Inc., 'Suicide, Self-Injury and Eating Disorders: Policy Details' (Web Page) <https://transparency.meta.com/en-gb/policies/community-standards/suicide-self-injury/>.

(Continued)

Annexure C (Continued)

<table>
<tr><th>Social Media</th><th>Policy Regarding Eating Disorder Content</th></tr>
<tr><td>Snapchat</td><td>'To promote safety, the following is prohibited on Snapchat:

Glorification of self-harm, including the promotion of self-injury, self-mutilation, suicide or eating disorders…Where users report content that indicates a risk of self-harm, our teams review these reports with an eye toward providing helpful resources and potentially identifying opportunities for emergency services to intervene, where possible. Additional information about our safety resources is available on our Privacy, Safety & Policy Hub.[2]</td></tr>
<tr><td>TikTok</td><td>'Disordered Eating and Body Image
We want TikTok to be a place that encourages self-esteem and does not promote negative social comparisons. We do not allow showing or promoting disordered eating and dangerous weight loss behaviors, or facilitating the trade or marketing of weight loss or muscle gain products.
Content is restricted (18 years and older) and ineligible for the For You Feed (FYF)[3] if it shows or promotes potentially harmful weight management, or markets weight loss or muscle gain products. Content is restricted (18 years and older), and ineligible for the FYF in some regions, if it shows cosmetic surgery and does not include risk warnings.
If you or someone you know is experiencing concerns about body image, food, or exercise, support is available. Contact a helpline in your region.
Disordered eating and dangerous weight loss behaviors means extreme dieting or fasting, or misusing medication or engaging in exercise for weight loss that may create a significant and immediate health or well-being risk.
Potentially harmful weight management means diets, medication, or exercise used for rapid or drastic weight loss or muscle gain that may create a long-term health or well-being risk.
…
NOT ALLOWED

• Showing, describing, promoting, or offering or requesting coaching for disordered eating or dangerous weight loss behaviors, including:
  • Extreme low-calorie diets
  • Bingeing and intentional vomiting
  • Misusing medication or supplements for weight loss
  • Exercising through serious injuries or illness
• Showing or promoting unhealthy body measurement and "body checking" trends, such as comparing body part size to household objects
• Facilitating the trade or marketing of weight loss or muscle gain products</td></tr>
</table>

[2] Snap Inc., 'Community Guidelines: Threats, Violence, & Harm' (Web Page, February 2025) <https://values.snap.com/policy/policy-community-guidelines/threats-violence-harm>.

[3] TikTok, 'For You Feed Eligibility Standards' (Web Page, 14 August 2025) <https://www.tiktok.com/community-guidelines/en/fyf-standards/>.

…

RESTRICTED (18 years and older)

- Showing, describing, promoting, or offering or requesting coaching for potentially harmful weight management behaviors including:
    - Restrictive low-calorie diets, such as extended intermittent fasting
    - Using medication or supplements for weight loss or muscle gain, such as anabolic steroid use
    - Exercises designed for rapid and significant weight loss, such as cardio routines that promise to help you lose a waist size in a week
- Promoting weight loss or muscle gain products, such as sharing a before-and-after transformation
- Promoting body types as ideal or perfect, when associated with potentially harmful weight management behaviors
- Showing or promoting cosmetic surgery that does not include risk warnings, including before-and-after images, videos of surgical procedures, and messages discussing elective cosmetic surgery

…

FYF INELIGIBLE

- Showing, describing, promoting, or offering or requesting coaching for potentially harmful weight management behaviors including:
    - Restrictive low-calorie diets, such as extended intermittent fasting
    - Using medication or supplements for weight loss or muscle gain, such as anabolic steroid use
    - Exercises designed for rapid and significant weight loss, such as cardio routines that promise to help you lose a waist size in a week
- Promoting weight loss or muscle gain products, such as sharing a before-and-after transformation
- Promoting body types as ideal or perfect, when associated with potentially harmful weight management behaviors
- Showing or promoting cosmetic surgery that does not include risk warnings, including before-and-after images, videos of surgical procedures, and messages discussing elective cosmetic surgery

…

ALLOWED

- Condemning disordered eating, dangerous weight loss behaviors, or potentially harmful weight management (as long as it does not show or describe a diet or behavior)
- Showing or describing:
    - Competitive eating contests, such as hot dog and pie-eating contests
    - Fitness routines and nutrition that are not primarily focused on extreme weight loss, such as preparing for competitive sports, marathon training, or body building competitions
    - Medically necessary surgery, such as including before-and-after images of the repair of a cleft lip, breast reconstruction after a mastectomy, or gender affirmation surgery
    - Medically necessary health interventions under the guidance of a medical or health professional, such as restrictive diets before surgery
    - Religious diet behavior and fasting
    - Physical disabilities and differently-abled bodies[4]

[4] TikTok, 'Mental and Behavioral Health' (Web Page, 17 April 2024) <https://www.tiktok.com/community-guidelines/en/mental-behavioral-health#2>.

(Continued)

Annexure C (Continued)

Social Media	*Policy Regarding Eating Disorder Content*
X	**'You may not promote or encourage suicide or self-harm.** At X, we recognize that suicide and self-harm are significant social & public health challenges that require collaboration between all stakeholders – public, private, and civil society – and that we have a role and responsibility to help people access and receive support when they need it… Under this policy, you can't promote, or otherwise encourage, suicide or self-harm. We define promotion and encouragement to include statements such as "the most effective", "the easiest", "the best", "the most successful", "you should", "why don't you". Violations of this policy can occur via Posts, images or videos, including live video. We define suicide to be the act of taking one's own life. We define self-harm to include: • self-inflicted physical injuries e.g., cutting; and • eating disorders e.g., bulimia, anorexia.[5]
YouTube	'At YouTube, we take the health and well-being of all our creators and viewers seriously. Awareness and understanding of mental health is important and we support creators sharing their stories, such as posting content discussing their experiences with depression, self-harm, eating disorders, or other mental health issues. However, we do not allow content on YouTube that promotes suicide, self-harm, or eating disorders, that is intended to shock or disgust, or that poses a considerable risk to viewers… If you are depressed, having thoughts of suicide, self-harming, or experiencing an eating disorder, know there is help and you're not alone. While coping with painful emotions, many people might experience these issues. Talking to a mental health care provider can help determine if you have a mental illness that requires care. It can also help you identify healthy, effective coping strategies and develop skills to manage difficult feelings. **Suicide and self-harm support resources** Below is a list of organizations dedicated to helping those in need in different countries and regions. These are recognised crisis service partners. Partnerships vary by country/region… YouTube users should not be afraid to speak openly about the topics of mental health, suicide, self-harm, and eating disorders in a supportive and non-harmful way. However, there are times when content is created that is sensitive and may pose a risk for some users. When you create content that contains suicide, self-harm, or eating disorder related topics, take into account the possible negative impact of your content on other users, especially minors and users who may be sensitive to this content… **Don't post the following content:** • Content promoting or glorifying suicide, self-harm, or eating disorders • Instructions on how to die by suicide, engage in self-harm, or engage in eating disorders (including how to conceal them) • Content related to suicide, self-harm, or eating disorders that is targeted at minors… In some cases we may restrict, rather than remove, suicide, self-harm, or eating disorder content if it meets one or more of the following criteria (for example, by placing an age-restriction, a warning, or a Crisis Resource Panel on the video)… If your content violates this policy, we will remove the content and send you an email to let you know. If we can't verify that a link you post is safe, we may remove the link. Note that violative URLs posted within the video itself or in the video's metadata may result in the video being removed.[6]

[5] X, 'X's Suicide & Self-Harm Policy' (Web Page) <https://help.x.com/en/rules-and-policies/glorifying-self-harm>.

[6] YouTube, 'Suicide, Self-Harm, and Eating Disorders Policy' (Web Page) <https://support.google.com/youtube/answer/2802245?hl=en>.

Annexure D Topics That This Book Discusses That Could Benefit from More Research

Topic	*Chapter in This Book That Discusses This Issue*	*Why More Research on This Topic Could Be Beneficial*
How seeing images of women with 'slim-thick' bodies impacts women	1	To make decisions on whether, potentially, Body Image Law should be amended to address the repercussions of seeing images of 'slim-thick' women
Body Image Law in the male context	2	To potentially be able to create a Body Image Law that results in positive outcomes for male body image or else modify existing Body Image Law so that it also tries to improve male body image
The impact of politicians giving awards to people and businesses to take positive actions regarding body image	4	If it is successful, then it might be useful to consider whether to amend Body Image Law to include this as another way to try to improve body image
The outcome on body image and eating disorders of businesses that decided (on their own, without government pressure) to take positive action related to body image	4	If it is having a positive impact, then this could encourage other businesses to create similar policies and possibly eliminate the need for Body Image Law entirely
The effect of the Body Image Laws in Israel, France and Norway	5	This could help politicians in Israel, France and Norway to understand whether they should leave their Body Image Laws as they currently are or modify or repeal the Laws and it could help politicians in other jurisdictions decide whether they should pass similar laws; it can also provide helpful evidence for Body Image Law advocates to use to try to convince politicians in countries where there is no Body Image Law to create one

(*Continued*)

Annexure D (Continued)

Topic	*Chapter in This Book That Discusses This Issue*	*Why More Research on This Topic Could Be Beneficial*
The impact on models' health of the Californian Law to give information on nutrition and eating disorders to models	5	This could help politicians in other jurisdictions consider if they should pass a similar law or whether to modify existing Body Image Law to include this measure
How to modify Body Image Law so that it can help to improve the health of models	5	This could help to accomplish a potential new aim of Body Image Law, to improve models' health
What would constitute diversity among models that would be best for the body image of viewers	7	This information could be used to amend existing Body Image Law or create new evidence-based Body Image Law that requires diversity among models
The impact of disclaimers on images that artificial intelligence made that state that artificial intelligence made the images on the body image of viewers (including the impact of the part of the 2023 French Influencer Law that requires such a disclaimer)	9	This information could be helpful to decide whether and how Body Image Law should be modified to address the thin-ideal models that artificial intelligence created in advertisements

Annexure E: A List of All Scholarly Work That the Author Could Find That She Believes Is Primarily about Body Image Law or Similar Policy

Attrill PA, 'Towards the Development of Photoshop Law and Its Enforceability within the European Union' (Masters Thesis, Tallinn University of Technology, 2023).

Baffsky R, 'Eating Disorders in Australia: A Commentary on the Need to Address Stigma' (2020) 8(1) *Journal of Eating Disorders* 1.

Bildfell C, 'Legislating Away Illness: Examining Efforts to Curb the Development of Eating Disorders through Law' (2018) 26 *Dalhousie Journal of Legal Studies* 37.

Bromberg M and Halliwell C, '"All About That Bass" and Photoshopping a Model's Waist: Introducing Body Image Law' (2016) 18 *Notre Dame Law Review* 1.

Bromberg M and Cardaci N, 'Feel[ing] Unpretty Too: Do Body Image Laws Measure Up in the Post COVID-19 World?' (2022) 22(1) *The Journal of Law in Society* 94.

Bromberg M, Hay M, Fitzgerald T and de Freitas C, '"You Are Beautiful No Matter What They Say": Applying an Evidence-Based Approach to Body Image Law' (2019) 34(1) *Issues in Law and Medicine* 183.

Cohen M and Latzer Y, 'The Impact of Israel's "Models' Law" on Young Women' (2021) 13(4) *International Journal of Psychological Studies* 32.

de Freitas C, Jordan H and Hughes EK, 'Body Image Diversity in the Media: A Content Analysis of Women's Fashion Magazines' (2018) 29(3) *Health Promotion Journal of Australia* 251.

Gauvin L and Steiger H, 'Overcoming the Unhealthy Pursuit of Thinness: Reaction to the Québec Charter for a Healthy and Diverse Body Image' (2012) 102(8) *American Journal of Public Health* 1600.

Gladstone J, 'The Skinny on BMI-Based Hiring: An Assessment of the Legality and Effectiveness of Israel's Weight Restriction Law' (2016) 15(3) *Washington University Global Studies Law Review* 495.

Hildesheimer G and Gur-Arie H, 'Just Modeling? The Modeling Industry, Eating Disorders, and the Law' (2015) 8(2) *International Journal of Feminist Approaches to Bioethics* 103.

Islam F, 'Promoting Healthy Body Images in Populations: Does Body Dissatisfaction Influence Reactions to Quebec's Charter for Healthy and Diverse Body Image?' (Masters Thesis, Université de Montréal, 2018).

Krawitz M, 'Beauty is Only Photoshop Deep: Legislating Models' BMIs and Photoshopping Images' (2014) 21(4) *Journal of Law and Medicine* 859.

Latzer Y, Adatto R and Neumark-Sztainer D, 'Addressing Eating Disorders through Legislation: The Israeli "Models' Law" – Process, Enactment, and Dilemmas' (2022) 1 *Dialogues in Health* 1.

McBride C et al, 'Digital Manipulation of Images of Models' Appearance in Advertising: Strategies for Action through Law and Corporate Social Responsibility Incentives to Protect Public Health' (2019) 45 *American Journal of Law & Medicine* 7.

Meyers EE, 'Fashioning Worker Protections to Combat the Thin Ideal's Cost on Fashion Models and Public Health' (2020) 20 *Vanderbilt Journal of Entertainment and Technology Law* 1219.

Reid Boyd E and Moncrieff-Boyd J, 'Swimsuit Issues: Promoting Positive Body Image in Young Women's Magazines' (2011) 22(2) *Health Promotion Journal of Australia* 102.

Rodgers RF and Laveway K, 'Retouchée au Féminin: The Gendered Nature of the French Law Mandating Labeling of Digitally Modified Images' (2021) 10(62) *Laws* 1.

Rodgers RF et al, 'Disordered Eating Behaviors and Sexual Objectification during New York Fashion Week: Implementation of Industry Policies and Legislation' (2021) 54(3) *The International Journal of Eating Disorders* 433.

Soltis CA, 'Dying to Be a Supermodel: Can Requiring a Healthy BMI Be Fashionable?' (2009) 26(1) *The Journal of Contemporary Health Law and Policy* 49.

Stuart M, 'Failure to Influence: Legislation Requiring Social Media Influencers to Disclose their Retouched Images will not Address Youth Body Image Concerns' (2024) 31(2) *University of Miami International and Comparative Law Review* 463.

Tschannen AC, 'An Argument for Incentivizing Voluntary Regulation of the Fashion and Modeling Industries' (2014) 6(2) *Washington University Jurisprudence Review* 421.

Index

For Product Safety Concerns and Information please contact our EU representative GPSR@taylorandfrancis.com Taylor & Francis Verlag GmbH, Kaufingerstraße 24, 80331 München, Germany

Printed and bound by CPI Group (UK) Ltd, Croydon, CR0 4YY
14/09/2026
02216243-0014